Lurcher and Long Dog Training

By the same author

The Complete Book of Sight Hounds, Long Dogs and Lurchers
Secrets of Dog Training

LURCHER AND LONG DOG TRAINING

D. Brian Plummer

ROBINSON PUBLISHING
London

Robinson Publishing
7 Kensington Church Court
London W8 4SP

First published by Robinson Publishing 1993

A copy of the British Library Cataloguing in Publication Data
for this title is available from the British Library.

ISBN 1 85487 238 9

Typeset by Hewer Text Composition Services, Edinburgh
Printed and bound in Great Britain by Mackays, Chatham

Contents

1

Exactly What Do You Want the Dog to Do?

David Hancock of Sutton Coldfield is probably the world's largest breeder of collie lurchers. He is certainly one of the most successful breeders, as the results of the national trials attest. Life at his home has however assumed the nature of a torture designed by someone who considered that the punishments of Tantalus, Prometheus and the stone-toting Sisyphus were not severe enough, for there are few moments of the day when the phone doesn't ring and a caller engages David in a lengthy session of questioning about the stock he has for sale. Over the years David has developed a technique to deal with such interrogations – an ingenious method of identifying clients who will not be satisfied with the type of stock Hancock breeds. As soon as the potential client enquires as to the stock David has on offer David counters with the question, 'What exactly do you require the dog to do?' If the buyer states that he simply wishes to walk the fields dog on slip and release the animal as soon as the hare leaves its form and springs into flight, Hancock stops the potential customer by saying, 'You don't require a lurcher. What you want is a saluki or a pure bred greyhound or a saluki/greyhound long dog. What I have to sell is not suitable for your needs.'

If however the would-be purchaser replies that he requires a dog to hunt rabbits, feathered game, to work alongside or with (there is a difference) ferrets, to catch game with the aid of a lamp or spotlight and, wonder of wonders, to work the dog in conjunction with a long net – the ultimate test of a lurcher trainer's skill, Hancock tells the would-be buyer of the stock he has for sale and probably even advises on the type of hybrid best suited to the client's requirements.

The fact is that despite the similar appearance of a lurcher to a long dog – both have a decidedly greyhoundy appearance, both are, or should be, capable of great speed approaching the velocity of a greyhound or whippet – there is, or should be, a vast difference between the roles required of the lurcher and the long dog. Long dogs are bred specifically to course hares, to have great speed and stamina to pursue the greatest mammalian athlete the Almighty has yet to create – the brown hare. Any rabbits a long dog catches should be regarded as a bonus by the coursing enthusiast as should any feathered game caught by the long dog.

The lurcher is, or should be, and we'll return to this subject at a later date, a rabbit catching dog, a dog capable of catching feathered game perhaps but seldom fast enough to course and catch a hare that is afforded fair law – any hares a true lurcher catches are usually taken by stealth or chance – or perhaps by a combination of both chance and stealth. It's a hoary old cliché but nevertheless an apt one, that a lurcher was originally developed (I am reluctant to use the expression 'was specifically bred') to be a potfiller, an animal that in addition to being a family dog would also fetch home rabbits, game birds and the occasional hare or so, hares taken by stealth as much as by speed, one should add. The lurcher was never intended to course hares given fair law, such a task is the prerogative of the pure bred sighthound, or by that result of mating two or more sighthounds together – the long dog.

Whether sighthounds are unintelligent or recalcitrant has long been debated. Many show a coursing 'cunning' that makes the observer question whether certain sighthounds are not amongst the most intelligent of domesticated canines. However one thing is certain: sighthounds and particularly the Middle Eastern sighthounds such as Afghan hounds, salukis and sloughis are some of the most intractable and difficult dogs to train. The Burgers, American circus dog trainers who include a band of Afghan hounds in their troupe of performing dogs, note that that their sighthounds take as much as six times as long to train as the more conventional breeds of dog such as poodles or terriers and the trainers must watch their sighthounds carefully to note when they are ready and willing to be trained. There are several, the late Michael Lyne and Paul Sagar come most readily to mind, who believe that this recalcitrance, that seems typical of the Middle Eastern hounds, could be attributed to the fact that these hounds mature more slowly and hence are seldom ready for serious obedience training, or obedience training for field work, before their fourth season.

Whether or not this is true of the sighthounds that constitute the group of hounds known as the Celtic group, the deerhound, the greyhound or the whippet, is debatable. Few obedience trainers consider sighthounds of any type to be suitable animals for training for competition. John Holmes, who achieved spectacular results with the training of a track/coursing bred greyhound, in the early 1950s – one hound scaled some 10 ft 6 ins at The Star Dog Tournament – makes no mention of the slow mental maturation of greyhounds though he had some difficulty adapting conventional methods of training to suit the hound. Indeed most greyhounds are considered to be over the top as athletes and put out to pasture (a delightful euphemism in the case of many old greyhounds) before they have reached the age when Lyne or Sagar considered the saluki to be arriving at an age when the breeder might expect the animal to be ready for serious training.

There is in fact some, albeit scant, evidence to suggest that the greyhound may be a great deal more intelligent than racers and coursers may credit the animals to be. Hancock of Sutton Coldfield, who has considerable experience with top class over the top racing and coursing greyhounds, is of the opinion that the greyhound is not unintelligent. Many, or so Hancock believes, would, if subjected to early socialising and training, perform equally well at tests and field work as many of the super-saturated lurcher strains (lurchers with more than three-quarters of their genetic make up made up of sighthounds) and certainly better than the majority of saluki bred long dogs.

If pure bred sighthounds are not particularly intelligent or not particularly tractable then neither are the long dogs bred by mating these sighthounds together. It has been said that saluki bred long dogs gain some intelligence through their mixed ancestry – perhaps indeed this certain 'something' may be associated with the quality known as hybrid vigour – mules are reputed to be more perspicacious than either horses or donkeys but few saluki hybrids are more trainable than pure bred coursing greyhounds or coursing bred whippets.

Long dogs, the result of cross-breeding between sighthounds, with no base blood, collie, Bedlington, retriever, GSD and so on, are seldom easy to train or as versatile and intelligent as are lurchers which have a strong trace of base blood.

Lurchers should in fact be bred to be versatile and intelligent as much as speedy. Indeed historical evidence does tend to show that the traditional lurcher of the eighteenth and nineteenth century (there is little evidence to suggest that lurchers were commonly kept before the eighteenth century simply because the rabbit, the staple quarry of the lurcher, was seldom encountered in a feral state before that date – and neither were pheasants or partridge reared in number before this time) was usually only a half-bred greyhound, the result of mating a greyhound to some form of pastoral dog or at the most a three-quarter bred greyhound with sufficient speed to catch hares as well as rabbits. The lurcher mentioned by Frederick Rolfe whose diary *I Walked By Night* was so carefully edited and pruned by Lilias Rider Haggard, was a cross between the blue shag sheepdog (one of the many varieties of bearded collie/Old English sheepdog bred in the East Anglian counties) and a greyhound, while Trapman's lurcher had an additional dose of greyhound or sighthound blood added to the half-bred mix. There is indeed a move afoot not to call an animal with more than three-quarters of its breeding greyhound or sighthound blood a lurcher. How those who suggest this believe it should be implemented has yet to be disclosed. Certainly it appears as if it is fair to say that a very fast lurcher is seldom a very intelligent lurcher, it invariably has too much sighthound in its make up. Furthermore a lurcher, no matter how it is infused with more and more sighthound blood, is seldom as efficient at fair-law coursing either under rules or in single dog matches as is a properly bred long dog or pure bred sighthound.

Hybrids between lurchers and long dogs would therefore on first impressions appear to be an ideal mixture, a priceless chimaera capable of catching hares and rabbits with equal alacrity, having the speed and endurance of a topgrade long dog and the stealth and versatility of the best type of lurcher. Nothing could be further from the truth. Long dog blood should be kept clear of lurcher bloodlines and there is every evidence to suggest that the only sighthound blood a true lurcher should have in its veins should be the blood of the coursing or racing greyhound. Saluki blood invariably produces a recalcitrant type of lurcher that tends to be less tractable and less versatile than the conventionally bred greyhound lurcher. The now very popular whippet/greyhound long dog, produced either as a by-product of a breeding project to produce more speedy racing whippets, or deliberately bred to produce a single-handed coursing dog, are unsuitable for mating to working lurchers simply because the crossbred produces such an incredible variety of sizes in a litter. Puppies from such unions can grow into giants approaching the size of a pure bred coursing greyhound or to tiny mites little larger than a show bred whippet. Deerhound blood, and once the deerhound/greyhound was the most popular long dog in Britain, adds little to the worth of a working lurcher for a deerhound is by definition simply a large hirsute greyhound – though it is certainly neither as speedy nor as fine a courser as a good greyhound.

Thus on the surface of it a buyer has to choose whether he wants a long dog or a lurcher, or more to the point, whether he wants a dog to be a hare courser which catches the odd rabbit or a rabbit hunting dog that will under the right circumstances bring down the occasional hare. Should the sportsman want a lurcher that will respond to training to a degree in excess of simply running a dog off a slip – and the majority of lurcher trainers are capable of little more than this – then he would be wise to select a dog that has a strong base line, that is, a three-quarter greyhound or even a lurcher with less greyhound blood. Saluki blood should be kept well clear of the blood of a working lurcher strain, and the presence of saluki blood in a strain of lurcher indicates that the breeder does not require a particularly obedient or versatile dog, or that the breeder is unaware of the peculiarities such sighthounds can introduce into a strain of lurcher.

It is a sad indictment on the type of person that the image of the lurcher attracts that most lurchers are extremely badly trained – so badly trained that breeders and trainers of other sporting breeds of dog hold the lurcher trainer in a great deal of contempt. This is not simply because many lurcher enthusiasts have a cavalier attitude towards both the countryside and landowner, but because the majority of lurcher owners own half-trained, ill-mannered brutes, virtually poor-grade greyhounds with far too much sighthound blood to allow the animals to be biddable, and 'trained' to a degree of obedience that makes the animal a menace to own, a nuisance rather than a pleasure to the owner. Such animals are simply kept on leashes, slipped at hares when a hare springs underfoot and if the dog puts up even a creditable show at coursing the hare the owner seems well pleased with the dog's performance. That the dog returns to hand half-heartedly, or only when it is ready to do so, escapes many lurcher owners who are quite content to allow their dogs to run not only any game the dog encounters but to run riot once they are released from their slip. These self-same trainers are, however, the very first to bleat that landowners are reluctant to allow lurchers on their fields. Frankly I have every sympathy with the landowner for, for every well trained lurcher I see, I encounter ten or more lurchers that would be an embarrassment to own.

It is to remedy this condition, or to elevate the image of the country sportsman, that the National Lurcher Racing Club chairman John O'Keeffe set to and devised a National Lurcher Racing Club Field Trial – a field trial that consisted of a preliminary obedience test to sort out the sheep from the goats, and there are all too many goats amongst the lurcher fraternity. The second test consists of a field trial where the competitors, who are winners of the obedience tests, are required to test the field skills of their dogs. O'Keeffe has been the subject of some criticism for insisting that an obedience test preceded the field trial – the true test of a lurcher. However there is great wisdom in O'Keeffe's system of selection. If the obedience test had not culled out the vast band of poor trainers who keep near lunatic unsteady lurchers, the field event would have attracted an enormous band of half-witted demented louts of the type that brought an end to the Lambourn Lurcher Show, at one time the top country sport event of September. O'Keeffe's trial – for such it is now called – will in time bring at least some credibility to lurcher owners and much needed parity to the lurcher, the breed of dog that is held in low esteem by owners of other hunting dogs.

To compete in O'Keeffe's trials a dog must have a fairly strong base line to be able to qualify for the field event – indeed in O'Keeffe's first trial Scotland fielded a three-quarter collie/greyhound, England a half-bred collie/greyhound and Wales a half-bred GSD/greyhound (at the time of writing Ireland is yet to select its obedience trial winner), so it would appear that anyone requiring a lurcher to compete in these events would do well not to seek out a dog with nearly pure sighthound ancestry – and frankly lurchers without a strong base line are not expected to perform well in the field tests either.

Thus while the hare courser should seek out fleet dogs with a large percentage of sighthound blood (or better still conventionally bred long dogs) to hunt his chosen quarry, the lurcherman, who requires a more biddable versatile dog, must seek out dogs with a strong base line. Here however is the rub. The majority of dogs advertised boast utterly spurious pedigrees and have been produced without the slightest regard for either brains or other qualities the puppies might have. I reach for my copy of *Shooting News*, the bible of the lurcher enthusiast, and read 'Deerhound/greyhound/Bedlington/greyhound/deerhound/greyhound/greyhound'. The animal, if the pedigree is true – and it most certainly is not –

has a mere one-eighth part base blood (the Bedlington is the only non-sighthound in the supposed pedigree) and hence one might expect a fairly fleet but scarcely biddable puppy from such a union.

The problem is that lurchers are so often bought, sold, swapped and traded that authentic pedigrees have long since been lost and spurious pedigrees are invented on the spur of the moment. Those pedigrees might be varied as and when the vendor decided it is expedient to do so. For instance, if the vendor finds his wares advertised as deerhound/greyhound/deerhound/greyhound/deerhound/whippet/greyhound/Bedlington terrier do not sell well, he is entitled, or rather, is able, to advertise the whelps as collie/greyhound/greyhound/Alsatian(GSD)/greyhound. Many vendors preface their advertisements with 'Genuine', for example, 'Genuine deerhound/greyhound/saluki/collie' which means that the vendor genuinely believes that the puppies he has for sale are 'genuinely' bred the way the advertiser has stated. This advertisement offers no guarantee whatsoever. It should be pointed out that the mental hospitals are choc-a-bloc with people who genuinely believe they are Napoleon — yet not one is the genuine Corsican tyrant.

Thus the lurcher owner who wishes to buy a genuine working lurcher with not too much sighthound in its ancestry is in a quandary and his quandary is exacerbated by the fact that the majority of lurcher breeders coming into possession of a bitch of doubtful origin are wont to breed from the said bitch and mate the creature no matter what its shape, no matter what the supposed origin, no matter what qualities the said animal may possess, to a pure bred greyhound. Hence good useful strains of lurcher — and reader, they did exist at one time — are diluted with sighthound blood until they are virtually pure bred sighthounds.

The would-be buyer of a working lurcher should therefore choose his puppy with care, bearing in mind that most dogs with a dash of greyhound blood are fast enough to catch a rabbit and the majority of puppies offered for sale are too sighthound saturated to be biddable. My ideal lurcher would be a greyhoundy dog with a collie's tractability and intelligence. However, Labradors, golden retrievers, spaniels, GSDs are also suitable base lines for lurcher breeding but ideally no lurcher which is required to absorb a degree of advanced training should have less than a quarter of its genetic make up made up of base or non-sighthound blood. A

super-saturated lurcher with more than three-quarters of its genetic make up made up of sighthounds, or sighthound composites, will seldom accept advanced training as readily as would a lurcher with a strong base line.

2

Why Train a Lurcher or
Long Dog anyway?

If a sighthound or a sighthound hybrid with only a tiny amount
of sighthound blood is taken into the field and slipped at a hare or
rabbit most of these dogs will run and attempt to catch the quarry.
If the dog is regularly slipped at a rabbit or hare sooner or later the
dog will catch its prey. Little or no encouragement and absolutely
no training is required to force the dog to chase. Ten or twenty
thousand years of breeding from dogs with a natural inclination to
course any small moving animal will have produced a dog that has
to be restrained rather than encouraged to course quarry. Thus, as
the sole purpose of owning a lurcher or a long dog is to course and
catch game, why then should it be necessary to give the animal any
training whatsoever? Indeed the majority of lurchers are given little
or no training as a visit to a lurcher show all too clearly indicates.
The beauty class where the aesthetic qualities of this type of dog
are judged is well attended. The agility and obedience tests staged
at such a show seldom attract more than half a dozen exhibits, dogs
that often find the act of sitting to command, the act of jumping a
hurdle, a little too much for them and retrieving a dummy often
beyond their mental capabilities – and these are the best trained
lurchers at the show one would assume! The others paraded around
a showring far from the obedience tests are clearly incapable of
performing even the rudimentary tasks required of the obedience
competitors. Perhaps the reader believes I am a shade too harsh on
the lurchers and trainers parading around the showring, however
I assure you I am certainly not understating the capabilities of the
average lurcher trainer. If some of those lurchers, purporting to

be efficient hunting dogs, so much as slip their leashes and run free, a chaotic and embarrassing scene is likely to be enacted with the owner chasing a recalcitrant brute which is racing around the showground heedless of the pleas and entreaties of its owner and causing all manner of mischief while it runs free. In 1989 a terrier was attacked and killed by a free-running lurcher whose owner no doubt believed the animal to be a first-rate well trained hunting dog.

It can and, indeed, has been argued that many of these recalcitrant, untrained lurchers may not perform well in the agility and obedience rings, but perform superbly in the field. This is also woefully untrue. The majority of lurchers are an embarrassment in the field as well as the showground. Far too many are unbroken to stock and hence are a nightmare to hunt in country where sheep or free-range poultry abound. Many lurchers are absolute liabilities that are a menace to all forms of farm livestock. Many will not jump and need to be lifted over low sheep wire or fences. Few will sit, lie, stay or be steady with long and purse nets and what is even more baffling, few lurchers and long dogs are steady with ferrets, and it takes little effort to train a lurcher to be steady with ferrets. Small wonder the lurcher trainer is held in contempt by the majority of fieldsport enthusiasts many of whom own and train superbly obedient dogs of other breeds.

What is more disturbing, however, is the spate of poor-grade illinformed writers who contribute to lurcher magazines and state that the teaching of a lurcher to sit, lie and stay and retrieve to hand any object the dog is sent to fetch constitutes teaching the dog pointless tricks that are useless in the field and valueless to the hunter. Now, such statements are clearly ludicrous as any thinking lurcherman will see.

Why, however, should a lurcher be taught to sit, lie and stay when all its owner require of the dog is to run and catch rabbits and hares? I have used the following example of why it is essential to have control over any breed of dog in other books but I make no apology for repeating the tale yet again. Rabbits seldom live in lush pastures and fertile water meadows but prefer dry pasture which they invariably have to share with sheep. Thus one day the lurcherman with lurcher at heel, or perhaps tugging madly on the leash might be more typical, approaches a rough pasture and observes an ewe with its head jammed in a space in the sheep wire. As the lurcherman approaches the ewe, the sight of the dog panics the animal, and the ewe stupid as all sheep are prone to be, proceeds to garotte itself. Each time the man approaches the sheep, the dog, excited by the furious struggles of the ewe, pulls forward to investigate and thereby increases the furious struggles of the trapped animal. If the dog could be put at a sit position, and made to stay put on command, the lurcherman would be able to move forward and extricate the now much calmer animal from the desperate plight in which the sheep has placed itself. As it is, the sheep continues to struggle and eventually strangles itself, for its struggles were increased four-fold by the presence of an inquisitive dog.

However, the lurcherman does not need to venture into the countryside with any regularity to justify teaching a dog to sit, lie, stay on command. It is not an uncommon sight to see a lurcher towing its owner around the average housing estate. The dog decides when and where the owner will cross the road and, if the lurcher decides to pursue a cat, a lurcher the size of a small greyhound is more than capable of towing its owner in front of a passing car. Yet if such a dog is trained it can be stationed at the kerbside and immobilised while its owner decides it is safe to cross the road.

An incident witnessed at Whaddon Chase in 1981 would have convinced any lurcher owner of the value of training a dog to remain immobile when its owner decides it should do so. It is rare to find a cynophobe, a person who is frightened of dogs, at any country show for these shows attract people who are interested in matters canine. A child fell and panicked when a group of lurchers, tails admittedly wagging, approached the prostrate infant. The more the child panicked the more friendly interest the lurchers paid to the infant while a distraught mother, equally frightened of dogs, so it appeared, pleaded with the owners to call their dogs to hand. If the dogs had been dropped at a distance from the child, the mother could have retrieved her distraught infant a great deal more easily than she did. Admittedly, no lurcher showed the slightest animosity to the child for few sighthound hybrids have a reputation for being biters, but in a country where attacks from large and ferocious dogs have alienated the general public from dog owners, more children are deliberately encouraged to be wary of large dogs than ever before. 'Don't take sweets from strangers and avoid large dogs', seems to be the dictum of the population of the once dog-loving Britain.

However in the hunting field the lurcherman needs considerable control over his ward. A dog wandering on top of an occupied burrow, or worse still, drifting off to explore other sights while the ferreter nets up, can be a confounded nuisance, not only can the dog's feet snag nets but the sound of the dog's footfall can alert the rabbit to the dangers that await it should the rabbit decide to bolt. A dog quietly stationed in the sit, lie position near the burrow while the ferreter nets up (a ferreting dog should be frozen rather that sat or put at a down position when rabbits begin to bolt before the ferret) causes far less disturbance than a dog allowed to wander noisily around the warren digging at any hole it pleases while the ferreter attempts to net up the burrow. A trained dog walking 'tippy-toe' across the top of the burrow seldom causes the rabbit to refuse to bolt but during the initial training programme a ferreter's dog should be encouraged to sit, lie or stay on command while its owner places the nets. It also goes without saying that a long netter's dog (and many consider lurchers an unsuitable aid to long netting) must always be under control and should stay put where the handler places it.

Yet more amazing still is the fact that few lurchers are taught to jump, for to teach such an athletic dog as a lurcher or a long dog to jump is simplicity itself. Shortly after Lambourn lurcher show triggered off the lurcher boom and just about every country show provided classes for lurcher enthusiasts, some enterprising, but ill-informed, show organisers decided that instead of organising lurcher races over a distance that would not tax the stamina of a whippet, they would place hurdles similar in height to the hurdles used in AAA 100 metre events along the track. Such a course has been run by poodle clubs and even by the Dandie Dinmont Club at one time, yet few lurchers competed in these classes, and those which did competed very badly, and often refused to jump.

Yet a lurcher needs to jump to be an effective hunting dog and nothing looks more absurd than the sight of a lurcherman helping his athletic ward over styles and sheep netting. I have related the following tale before, yet I make no apology for repeating it. Some years ago I was invited to witness the performance of one of those long dogs against which no hare could endure, the sort of paragon that deals out death and destruction to every hare it supposedly encounters. Such wonderful animals are sought as eagerly as the waters of eternal youth, but, to date, I have yet to encounter one. What I was to encounter was, however, an amazing double act, the like of which I've never seen since.

A hare sprung underfoot and the long dog owner, a stocky, powerfully built man, promptly slipped his dog and then ran mightily after the long dog. When the dog encountered its first fence it raced up and down the fence, seeking a gap through which it could squeeze. Its owner, who had now arrived at the fence, promptly seized the long dog and hurled it over the fence, whereupon the course continued, dog in pursuit of the hare and man in pursuit of the dog! Several fences were negotiated in the way so described and, needless to say, the hare escaped capture. I still marvel at the speed and stamina of the thickset, powerfully built man, though the athletic prowess of the dog proved a little less than impressive. If the dog had been taught to jump, the hare might have been caught, or better still, if the man had taken professional coaching, he could have dispensed with the services of the dog! Nevertheless, the bizarre scene is indelibly imprinted in my mind.

It is commonly believed in Caithness, allegedly the home of some of the best trained collies and the very worst trained lurchers, that once a non-jumping dog has chased its first hare the dog can never be taught to jump 'on the run', or to leap fences while coursing, in every day parlance. This is nonsense though the reasoning behind the statement is easy to understand. Caithness is the most northerly province on the British mainland and for some reason whenever a lurcher is found to be unsatisfactory it passes further and further north until the very worst, most dispirited, physically and mentally damaged dogs come to rest in Caithness. These animals have known a few dozen owners, each one less caring than the last. These lurchers and long dogs often arrive in Caithness having lost much of their confidence, and are correspondingly more difficult to train than a well-adjusted, unspoilt young lurcher would be. Yet even the most broken-down, dispirited, oft-swapped lurcher or long dog can be taught to jump on the run, and even perform this feat in Caithness!

It is, however, totally baffling as to why so many lurcher owners keep lurchers or long dogs that will not retrieve or simply catch and stand over their kills, but decline to return that catch to hand. It is even more baffling to hear lurcher enthusiasts claim that they do not require a lurcher or long dog to retrieve its catch to hand and are quite content if the dog simply catches its quarry. The lurcher owner is seemingly then required to walk to the dog to recover the catch. Should such a person keep a lurcher to be a companion dog to ensure its owner stays fit, a non-retrieving lurcher is the very best animal to own. If the dog is a proficient catcher of rabbits or of hares then its owner will soon boast the stamina, physique and endurance of Emile Zatopek, simply by dint of constantly running out to collect 'downed' game the dog has caught but declined to retrieve. There is yet another tale, yet another Caithnessian tale (and lurcher lore boasts many Caithnessian tales) of a lurcher enthusiast who had once been a physical training instructor who came to Caithness to hunt. He was approached by one Caithnessian aficionado whose conversation went something like this, 'See this dog, he don't retrieve, so I takes Jack (a burly friend) with me. Shine beam, slip dog. Whoosh, dog has rabbit in mouth – Jack fetches it. Another rabbit, whoosh, dog has it, never misses, "Jack, fetch it". Some nights we takes a hundred rabbits. I bet you'd like to have this dog.' The PE instructor eyed the fool telling the tale and replied, 'I'd rather have Jack to train for the next Olympic Games.' Indeed Jack must have been a physical marvel for he would have run more than twelve miles at a speed apparently approaching that achieved by a greyhound to have achieved such a feat.

Yet training even the most super-saturated lurcher (a lurcher with seven-eighths or more sighthound blood) or a long dog with no base blood to retrieve is simplicity itself and many lurchers retrieve to hand and with absolutely no training, one should add.

Both lurchers and long dogs share the dubious distinction of being the worst trained animals of dogdom. It is not uncommon to find lurchers which do not sit, lie or stay, that are non-retrievers and refuse to jump; some are absolute devils with livestock and pursue sheep and hares with equal alacrity. Not surprisingly, the lurcher is unwelcome on most land, not because it is the filcher of game, the insignia of the moucher, that shadowy rustic Autolycus figure, but simply because so many lurchers are so obviously out of control that they afford no confidence to the landowner that his livestock will be respected. Add to this non-jumping, non-retrieving, non-sitting, non-staying, the fact that many lurchers are slow or reluctant to come to hand when called. It is clear that such an animal must be a terrible embarrassment to its owner and as welcome to the country landowner as foot and mouth disease.

Yet, the lurcher is not a difficult breed or type of dog to teach any task.

3

Basic Training

So, having shown fairly conclusively that lurchers should be subjected to a training programme, rather than simply taken to a field and slipped at any quarry the lurcherman may consider suitable, what exactly does the lurcher need to be taught? Basically, lurcher training should be divided into two sections:

a) basic training – coming to hand on command, lead training, sit, lie, stay training, jumping, retrieving training and stock breaking.

b) field training – ferreting, lamping, coursing training, and this is the ultimate form of field training, teaching a dog to work a long net, and few lurchers are under control enough to perform this last task. Indeed, it can be argued quite logically that the very nature, disposition and qualities a lurcher manifests makes it unsuitable as a long netting dog, but we will return to this subject presently.

Any newcomer to the world of lurcher training I would advise to join an obedience training club and take expert tuition from qualified and competent handlers. Avoid the wisdom proffered at the beer tents in the lurcher shows like the plague. Much of the advice given is sheer hocus pocus or utter lunacy, offered by people many of whom would be unable to train a dog of any breed. A young man with his first lurcher can be easily influenced by the bizarre and colourful bands a lurcher show attracts, yet few of these people are either qualified or capable of giving advice to beginners. The tyro lurcherman would do well to note how many of the beer tent savants will proudly parade their wards around the showring requiring a judge to determine which is the prettiest dog, yet will be conspicuous by their absence at any event that requires a dog to be trained to any level of obedience, though many will enter their dogs in the lurcher racing, an event that requires little training of the dog and virtually no skill on the part of the lurcher owner.

The lurcher savants, self appointed experts with a host of exaggerated tales of the prowess of dogs they once owned, but oddly enough, no longer possess, are certainly not the sort of people to advise a youngster concerning the basic training skills that must precede the entering of a lurcher to quarry. Furthermore, the lurcher trainer must realise that once a dog that is not trained to a reasonable standard of obedience is allowed to hunt up quarry and become wed to chasing rabbits or hares, further basic obedience training becomes difficult, if not impossible, to achieve.

The tyro lurcherman must also reject tales of superb lurchers that were taken into the fields at twelve weeks of age, caught the first rabbits they encountered and went on to become legends. Better still, the sensible lurcherman would do well to note how many dogs that were supposedly catching rabbits before they were five months old are offered for sale before they are a year old simply because they have become difficult to train, impossible to control and mindful of only the game they see. If a dog is not obedience trained before it is entered to quarry it is unlikely it will profit from obedience training at a later date and will simply swell the numbers of untrained embarrassments found parading around the showring at summer lurcher shows. If I may offer an epigram to counter the ridiculous rubbish lurcher enthusiasts tell youngsters, it matters little how quickly a dog chases a rabbit, most lurchers will catch rabbits, but it matters a great deal how quickly the dog will return to hand. The tyro lurcherman must forget hunting until his hound has become obedient enough not to embarrass the owner once it is taken into the field.

The advantages the lurcher buff may gain from joining obedience training classes are many. Most classes are run by highly competent dog trainers, many of whom have an excellent knowledge of dog behaviour and will willingly impart that knowledge to the lurcher owner. Many dog training clubs have specialist equipment of which the lurcherman can avail himself and the better clubs often arrange events that help create great bonhomie amongst the club members. On the debit side, and alas there is one, few trainers have much knowledge of sighthounds or sighthound hybrids and have usually majored in breeds such as collies, GSDs and Labradors, breeds that learn far more quickly than sighthounds or sighthound composites. There is some evidence that sighthounds learn somewhat differently from other dogs and few professional dog trainers accept sighthounds for training, simply because sighthounds learn so slowly. However, the majority of trainers at good dog training clubs are intelligent, versatile and usually prepared to make allowances for the rate at which sighthounds and their hybrids learn certain tasks.

However many clubs are only prepared to take on puppies older than six months of age and the lurcher puppy must undergo an intensive training programme long before this age. It is, in fact, rather bad policy to buy sapling lurcher puppies that are older than six months old and have received no formal training and little socialising, though long dogs which are not required to be as versatile as lurchers are often sold at this age, for many breeders are unwilling to select the long dog of their choice until the puppies are at least six months old.

Victorian dog training manuals usually state that no puppy is ready for training until it is six months old. Perhaps the dog training clubs that suggest that six months is the age at which they are prepared to take a whelp say so because of the dictates of tradition (it is more likely done because the young whelp will cause a disturbance and upset a class of adult dogs).

Yet puppies can and should be taught a great many activities before they are six months old.

Puppies should begin their training programme as soon as they arrive at their new homes and, of course, the first lesson a puppy must learn is to answer to its name. The owner should decide on the puppy's name long before the whelp has spent its first night at its new quarters, and once the new owner has decided on the name they intend to call the puppy they should avoid changing the name from day to day, one day calling the whelp Gyp (lurcher owners are seldom original) and the next day Sam. Nothing could confuse a puppy more.

Once the owner has decided on the name he or she intends to call the whelp it is time to train the puppy to come to call when the name is uttered. This is an extremely easy skill to teach the puppy. Simply utter the puppy's name as one starts to feed the whelp and allow it to associate the clatter of the food bowl with the sound of its name. Similarly if the owner falls to his hands and knees, thereby bringing his face level with that of the puppy, and utters the puppy's name, the whelp will approach the owner to investigate the strange change of shape. If the owner rewards the puppy with effusive praise, 'Good boy Gyp/Sam', or better still, offers the whelp food when it comes to hand, the animal soon learns to associate the sound of Gyp or Sam with pleasure. Very young puppies are easily taught to come to hand by rattling the food bowl at feeding times and uttering the puppy's name. One GSD breeder I know quite well bred ten almost identical black and tan whelps which came to their names as soon as they heard them, long before the said puppies were old enough to leave the nest. Each puppy was given its own food dish and each puppy called by name to feed. I should expect even a saluki puppy to pay attention to its name within a day of it arriving at its new home, and salukis have a well earned reputation for recalcitrance.

Let us however digress a little and discuss the trainer's action of dropping to his hands and knees, calling the puppy and uttering the whelp's name as he does so. Why this action usually encourages a puppy to come to hand quickly and without question has been the subject of debate for many years. It has been suggested that face-to-face contact encourages a puppy to come and lick or nose the face of the trainer in the same way as puppies separated from the dam, or on greeting a strange but clearly not hostile dog for the first time, are wont to nose the face of their mother. Likewise it has been suggested that a human being towering over any puppy intimidates rather than affords the puppy the confidence it needs to encourage it to come to its human owner. A face near the floor and the human body maintained in a position other than upright is apparently less intimidating to the puppy. Babies crawling around floors certainly attract the attentions of young puppies, indeed, it is often very difficult to stop a young puppy pestering, licking and nosing the face of a young child crawling around the floor, its face level with that of the puppy. However, whatever the reason, falling to one's hands and knees certainly encourages the puppy to come to hand, and the trainer should utilise this means of encouraging the puppy to come to its name, whatever the reason for the reaction from the whelp.

Even though the puppy comes readily to hand, the trainer should unobtrusively continue with recall training for the rest of the dog's working life. When the dog is to be fed its name should be uttered, when the dog is being walked it should be called to hand from time to time and petted as its name is uttered. It must equate the sensation of pleasure with the sound of its name and it should never be called by name and punished when it comes to hand. This is

on it. It is however policy for the trainer to release the puppy after a particularly traumatic lead training session and engage the puppy in a wild game so that the training session does not end on a sour note. Ilan, my now aging lurcher stud dog, became very upset by each and every lead training session, so upset in fact that he needed to be coaxed to play. He took two weeks of two or three minutes a day of training sessions to lead break him, longer in fact than any of the family either before or after him.

The flopper is a totally different kettle of fish and I confess there have been times when I have despaired of ever getting a persistent flopper lead trained. My personal experience has led me to believe there is a higher incidence of floppers in lurchers with a strong baseline than in long dogs or super-saturated strains of lurcher. In fact the very worst flopper I've ever encountered while training lurchers was a black and white son of a Baliska Ban greyhound and an obedience trained collie. Tully, for so I called the animal, flopped immediately the choke-chain or collar was fitted and he did not wait for the lead to be attached. In fact he flopped as soon as he saw the choke, collar or lead appear. One day I sat for an hour, Tully on his back traumatised by the lead training session, wondering what the devil I should do next. Fortunately Tully had by this time developed an affinity with Fathom, an aging lurcher bitch, and rose to play with her when she appeared. I requested a friend walk Fathom up the path and Tully, still on the lead, trotted along behind her. After a week of this training Tully reluctantly agreed to walk on the leash, and I had no further trouble from him. I hasten to add that the flopping does not indicate the animal's lack of mental fortitude, far from it, for Tully was an extremely game animal. Flopping is indeed an extremely efficient method of the puppy passively fighting the leash.

If another dog is not readily available the flopper can sometimes be coaxed to its feet and the owner must then either coax the puppy to follow him or exert a gentle pressure on the lead while the owner walks off encouraging the puppy to follow him. The flopper will attempt to roll over or fall on its belly but the taut lead will prevent the whelp from doing so, and though the whelp will certainly dig in its heels and refuse to follow, the friction caused by the feet encountering the ground will convince the youngster it is more pleasant to follow than to dig in its heels.

A word of warning will not come amiss at this point. The tyro dog trainer should conduct his initial lead training session in private. The sight of a grown man or woman towing around a reluctant puppy or the vision of a puppy furiously attempting to fight the lead will upset someone – more than likely someone who has no knowledge of canine behaviour- and hushed whispers and anonymous phone calls will often result in either the police or an RSPCA official investigating allegations of cruelty. Clearly no cruelty has been committed but a visit from either police or RSPCA official can be upsetting to the dog trainer making his first tentative steps at lead breaking a whelp.

I view the sight of a dog happily bounding about when its owner reaches for the collar and chain with some pleasure. It is a clear indication the owner has lead trained the dog properly. The dog clearly associates the sight of the leash with a sensation of pleasure. A good dog trainer will endeavour to make every training experience pleasurable to the dog. The act of lead training is seldom pleasurable to either the dog or the trainer however. Hence a wild exciting romp must precede and follow a training session and it is perhaps wise for the trainer to carry a lead when he takes the dog on a ramble even though the trainer has no intention of using the lead. This will usually cause the dog to associate the sight of the lead with a pleasurable sensation. It is also wise to always exercise commonsense while training any type of dog to the lead. For instance, if a dog which is engaged in a wild romp is called to hand so that its owner and the dog might return home, the dog, on returning to hand, should never be placed on the lead without being petted, talked to and even given titbits so as to buffer the action of returning to hand and being placed on the lead with some activity the dog finds pleasurable. No training activity should ever be allowed to end on a sour note.

4

Sit, Lie, Stay Training

I believe I have already dispensed with the notion that it is pointless and demeaning to the lurcherman to teach his lurcher or long dog to sit, lie and stay. So, forthwith are the accounts of how to teach these hybrids to assume the aforementioned positions.

Personally I would never attempt to teach any dog to sit, lie or stay before the animal had been lead trained. If the animal is not lead trained it can, if it finds the training session not to its liking, 'cut and run' whenever it wishes. When the animal has been lead broken, and subsequently cannot escape from the restrictions imposed by its leash, further training can proceed at a rate determined by the trainer and not the puppy. It is simplicity itself to teach the puppy to sit long before it has been lead trained but it is considerably easier to teach the lead trained whelp the same exercise.

So let us assume that not only has the puppy been broken to the lead, but accepts the presence and restrictions imposed by the leash without complaint. Sit training automatically follows on from this state. Simply take the puppy on a leash, holding the leash in one hand and pressing down on the whelp's rump with the other hand, and utter the word, 'Sit', as one does so. Few puppies will actually enjoy the sit training session, but the tyro dog trainer will certainly be amazed at how quickly the whelp accepts the training and sits on command. If the whelp proceeds more quickly when the owner lavishes effusive praise or offers titbits as rewards then by all means use such methods to reinforce the puppy's reaction to the command, 'Sit'. Some puppies will learn to sit after a ten minute training session, others may take longer, for much depends on the nature of the whelp, the competence of the trainer and, above all, the reciprocity that exists between the whelp and the trainer. Incidentally, it helps if other dogs are not present during the training session and better still if the trainer is alone with the puppy.

There are of course other methods of teaching a dog to sit, and the following method is often as, or more, efficacious in teaching older dogs to obey the sit command.

The trainer, dog on leash, walks the lurcher along a route, stopping suddenly, swinging the body over the head of the dog, raising his right or left hand, whichever hand is not used to hold the leash, and uttering the command, 'Sit'. I have watched diminutive women train large and recalcitrant dogs quickly and efficiently using this method, but I confess I have seldom experienced great success using this technique. The fault, 'dear Brutus', is undoubtedly with me, not with the training method – it is simply a technique I have never managed to master properly and hence I invariably train a whelp by the forcing down of its rump method.

At one time I invariably followed sit training with down, or lie down, training, but the progression is fraught with problems as I shall explain presently. The majority of tyro dog trainers drop the dog to the sit position and then by pressing down the dog's shoulders and uttering the word, 'Down', or 'Lie', teach the lie position. It is admittedly easier to force an already sitting dog to the lie position, but dogs, and particularly sighthounds, are very much creatures of habit and, unlike man, expect A to be followed by B and B to always be followed by C. Hence the majority of dogs taught first to sit and then taught the down position while they are sitting, usually on assuming a sit position, promptly assume a down or lie position before they are commanded to do so. This is particularly the case of dogs that are left at the sit position for some length of time, for not only do such dogs anticipate being commanded to drop to the down position but they are more at ease and more comfortable when in the prone position anyway.

Modern trainers deliberately avoid placing the dog in the sit position and then pressuring the dog to down, and go to some pains to keep the two exercises separate. Down is taught by pressing the still standing puppy's shoulders, uttering the word, 'Down', as the puppy is pushed earthwards. Some trainers even buffer the sit training session from the down training method by a series of wild games or an exciting training session, so as not to confuse the dog with the nature of the two activities. Old training manuals invariably lumped both sit and down training together but dogs trained by dint of reference to these books are all too eager to anticipate owners' commands and to revert from sit to down before the command is given.

The down command is an extremely versatile one. Not only is the command used to fix an animal in a position or situation – when ferreting etc. – but the command, 'Down', has such an imperative nature about it that it is used to stop a lurcher in mid flight and in this respect it is far more efficacious than the command, 'Stop', 'Come here' or 'No' in checking the dog in its tracks. Police dogs throughout Europe and America are invariably taught 'Down' as a means of calling them off an attack – though the methods used to train this instant obedience would certainly not find favour with the majority of dog lovers. I am unwilling to mention how this instant response is taught in a book concerned with lurcher training, for such methods would not be suitable to train lurchers, long dogs or sighthounds and if used incorrectly would result in the production of a seriously deranged dog.

The down position now mastered, the logical progression would be to teach the dog the down/stay position which enables the dog to be left at the down position when the owner walks away from the prone dog and, eventually, walks out of sight of the animal which should not rise or strive to follow him. This section of the training programme may be a little more difficult to teach the dog than the tyro dog trainer may realise. At this point, however, it is efficacious to digress somewhat and explain that most baffling of control methods, namely eye contact.

It is believed that animals convey many messages by staring. Staring is in most species usually used as a warning from a high ranking member of a group of animals to a lesser ranking member of its own species. Staring is in fact used as a prelude to attack. Few dogs do not mentally wilt if a trainer fixes them with his eyes though it is often a dangerous practice when a trainer takes on a maladjusted, powerful dog, particularly one that has somehow achieved a position of dominance over its canine or human pack members. Sighthounds are seldom very assertive dogs and usually readily submit to any human being who displays a modicum of confidence. It is worth noting that the significance of staring has long been realised by human beings. Men who are unable to look a fellow man in the face while speaking to him are often treated as inferiors by their fellow humans. Kipling's Mowgli was banished from the wolfpack because the wolves could not tolerate his tendency to stare while he addressed other members of the Seeonee pack. However, the power of eye contact should be utilised when the trainer is teaching a young lurcher to remain in the down position.

The trainer should drop the dog to the down position and, while fixing the puppy with his eyes, back away from the puppy uttering the command, 'Down', if the puppy attempts to rise and follow him. Dogs are naturally gregarious and particularly when quite young suffer mentally if the owner looks like leaving them. Hence, a sighthound or lurcher puppy dropped to the down position and left while its owner backs away may become more than a little distressed by the action. It is wise not to move too far from the puppy – its behaviour should dictate just how far – during the first training sessions. Once the whelp has stayed at the down position for the period required of it the owner should return to the puppy and lavish a great deal of praise on the whelp. On no account should he call the whelp and praise the dog when it comes to him, for the puppy will then believe the owner is praising it for coming to hand rather than because it has stayed at the down position.

The distance between the handler and his puppy should be increased but increased gradually as the owner slowly backs away from the whelp while still fixing the puppy with his eyes. When the distance between the puppy and the handler has reached the stage where eye contact is obviously no longer effective, yet the whelp stays in the down position, the handler may consider that he is ready to embark on the next stage of the training programme.

The puppy is now left in the down position and the handler turns his back on the whelp repeating the 'Down' command as he walks perhaps ten paces from the puppy. The puppy now no longer fixed by the handler's eye contact will almost certainly rise to follow the handler, so the 'Down' command should be repeated as the handler walks away. One of the most efficient demonstrations of this training programme I have ever witnessed was given by a lady who strode away from her dog and uttered 'Down' exactly when the dog attempted to rise. It was almost as if the lady had developed a telepathic link with her dog, a link that allowed her to predict exactly when the dog was ready to rise and follow her. After a while I noticed she was carrying a tiny handmirror in her fist and observed the reflection of the dog as she walked away from it. It was a useful and clever training aid and one I have sometimes adopted when training puppies of all breeds.

The trainer must accustom the dog to remaining steady while the handler walks thirty or so paces away from the dog before proceeding to the next portion of the training programme – leaving the dog at the down position while the trainer passes out of sight of the dog. This is usually one of the most traumatic experiences the puppy will have encountered during its basic training programme and once the owner disappears from view its a racing certainty the puppy will rise and attempt to follow. It is in fact quite difficult to ensure the puppy does not rise and follow when the owner steps out of sight for the first time and my diaries reveal that not once have I been able to drop a lurcher puppy, walk out of view for the first time in the training programme, and still find the puppy in the position I left it when I returned a few seconds later. No training programme runs completely smoothly and in this portion of the training schedule the trainer must expect the puppy to either rise and attempt to follow him or, upset by the owner vanishing from view, creep forward on its belly to investigate where its owner has gone.

I've always found the best method of teaching a puppy to stay at the down position when I disappeared from view was to drop the dog to a down position and disappear behind a tree or corner and stay there pressed against the tree or wall. When the puppy attempts to follow me, and it always does, I step out from my hiding place, verbally scold the dog, take it back to its original down position and resume the training programme. I am perhaps a shade anthropomorphic when I say that I believe that all my dogs are convinced that when I vanish from view I am waiting behind the nearest corner or tree for the dog to break the down position.

This method works well, but it is wise for the lurcher trainer to practice this method of training in a deserted area, far from inquisitive dogs or people. The appearance of a strange dog of any age or breed will almost certainly cause the puppy to break from the down position and people are usually intensely suspicious of a grown man who places a dog in the down position and promptly hides behind a corner or tree. Frankly, such a sight is usually enough to convince anyone who has no experience of training a dog that the handler is a certifiable lunatic. I have twice been reported to the police while training a dog to stay at the down position while I walked out of sight. When one considers just how suspicious people are when they observe a dog trainer behaving in a manner they consider strange, it is amazing just how many burglaries are not observed by nosy neighbours.

However, once the dog has learned that it must stay at the down position when commanded and, more important still, that the trainer will eventually return and praise the dog, the handler should increase the periods spent away from the dog. Puppies and adults alike seldom enjoy this exercise so the owner would be wise to return to the dog at the end of each training session and engage the dog in a wild game and/or offer the dog profuse praise and food rewards.

Some dogs will apparently stay at the down position for a considerable length of time; in fact it is far easier to train a dog to stay down for a lengthy period of time than to keep a dog at sit for a like length of time. I am sceptical of tales of dogs kept at the down position for very long periods, however – tales of dogs down for two days smack of Robert Michael Ballantyne. As soon as a dog's bladder movements prompt the dog to move from the down position the dog's concentration is broken and the animal will endeavour to seek out its owner. Few lurcher owners would require a dog to stay at the down for such a period of time, shades of Greyfriars Bobby perhaps! The NLRC test does, in fact, require the dog to stay at the down position for only 30 seconds when the owner is out of sight.

5

Jumping Training

I have never enjoyed teaching a dog to stay at the down position for a long period of time, and neither have my dogs enjoyed this training programme. Jumping training is, or can be, enjoyable for both the dog and the trainer and I freely admit I really enjoy training a dog to jump. Many, many lurchers aren't trained to jump, and are hence relegated to the level of second-rate hunting dog because of their inability to follow game in fenced, hedged or walled country, but once a dog and owner have mastered the techniques involved during jumping training the activity can become as addictive as an opiate. Some years ago I owned a very athletic lurcher called Burke – he features many times in the pedigrees of my present line of lurcher. Burke's equal has never again been produced by my strain of lurcher and perhaps it was for the best, for Burke was an obsessive jumper. He tingled with excitement each time he saw a hurdle constructed and his excitement seemed to radiate up his leash and permeate my whole body until I too became as excited about the forthcoming event as he was – well not quite as excited for I believe Burke was slightly crazy.

As time went by, and to satisfy my own insufferable vanity, I competed in these popular jumping contests each week throughout the summer. He became a difficult animal to control when he saw the hurdles being constructed prior to the event taking place, or worse still, a dog actually jumping these hurdles. He would shriek and struggle to be jumping and as I could not control his enthusiasm he had to be taken far from the hurdles until we were ready to compete. He suffered some damage while jumping but even when injured he struggled valiantly to be back scaling and hurdling. Burke lived for jumping and eventually died jumping, breaking his neck when he leapt a hedge and landed on some antique farm machinery left on the far side of the hedge.

Even tiny puppies just out of the nest can be taught to jump, and I've seen some amazing embryonic jumpers that had yet to be weaned. If a board of, say, six inches in height is placed across the front of kennels, between kennels and the run, and the puppies called to their feed, even tiny puppies, mites less than six weeks of age, will scramble over the board to be fed. If a board of somewhat greater dimensions, a foot to fifteen inches, is substituted for the original board and the puppies called to feed, most will succeed in scrambling over the higher obstacle to be fed. I seldom encourage young puppies to attempt to scramble over very large obstructions as there is a probability of the whelps damaging their legs, pasterns and paws as they land on the hard surface of the run, but I have seen twelve-week-old puppies scramble up and over six feet high fencing on command.

As the puppy gets older it can be called over objects which are considerably higher and it is quite amazing to see how soon a youngster will learn the actual physical process of lifting its legs and bodies over obstructions. It is worth noting that while most puppies can be taught to leap or scramble over objects through which they cannot see, they often experience some confusion when they encounter wire fencing over which they are required to jump. When puppies that have hitherto leaped three feet wooden hurdles with some ease encounter a somewhat lower wire fence they will frequently run up and down such a fence in order to find a route through the wire. Hence the advocates of calling on jumping, as this jumping training method is often called, would do well to vary the type of hurdle over which they call their puppies. Wire netting obstructions should be substituted for wooden hurdles from time to time to accustom the whelp to jump any form of obstacles it may encounter during the course of a day's hunting.

Perhaps at this point it is wise to deal with the subject of barbed wire fences or sheep wire fences long the top of which is stretched a length of barbed wire, and such devices bring more dogs to grief than the reader imagines. Personally I dread these constructions and fear for both my dogs and myself when I encounter them. I often buffer the top strand by placing my arm across the strand and encouraging the dog to 'touch-jump' the fence, its hind legs touching my arm rather than the strand of barbed wire. If this is not to the reader's liking, and one could scarcely blame any reader who found it a shade disconcerting to stretch an arm across barbed wire, a jacket placed across the stretch of wire one expects the dog to jump will often prevent damage to the dog's hind legs. I take great care not to allow a puppy to become injured by wire and I confess my heart always misses a beat when I see even an adult lurcher leap an unguarded strand of wire. If the reader judges lurcher shows it may pay him to note just how many puppies and adult lurchers alike display faint scratch marks on the insides of their hind legs where a single tine has scratched the dog as it has endeavoured to leap a barbed wire fence. Some dogs learn a great deal after their first hurt from wire. Canaan, my saluki/greyhound long dog leaps wire fences of any sort with some trepidation, clearing the top strand by two feet or more, simply because she was scratched while leaping a barbed wire sheep fence. Other dogs which have been injured while jumping such fences will quit leaping sheep wire and resume the futile practice of running up and down the fence in order to find a gap through which they can crawl. The dangers barbed wire topped fences can produce cannot be over-estimated, particularly if the sheep wire is topped by a double strand of barbed wire. Fathom, a daughter of my great jumper Burke, was always careful of how she jumped sheep wire (and incidentally she lost a great many rabbits because of this excessive care) simply because her hind leg was once trapped between a double strand of wire on a sheep fence in Tamworth. She hung there a full thirty seconds screaming and snapping at my hands that were working to free her and ever after she approached sheep wire, with or without a topping of barbed wire, always with slight trepidation. At the time of writing I own a great great great granddaughter of this now ancient Fathom that is a foolhardy jumper of wire fences and attempts to jump them in a springbok style, her hind legs touching the top strand of the fence. It is only a matter of time before she is either seriously injured by her style of jumping or pricked slightly and adjusts her method of jumping the fences.

However if the lurcher keeper wishes to jump his dogs in one of the very fashionable jumping contests that are regularly staged at summer shows he would be advised to adopt another method of training his dog the action of jumping hurdles. This method of training, adopted by those who jump their dogs at competitions, is known as running up jumping and this method cannot be taught the nestling puppy that has not yet been lead trained. Though it does no harm to start the puppy by encouraging it to leap or scrabble over low obstacles to secure its food.

Running up jumping should never be taught until the whelp is not only lead trained but will quite happily accept the presence of a collar or choke chain around its neck. I must admit I really enjoy teaching a puppy to jump using this method, so perhaps the reader will forgive the fact that I may dwell for too long on the subject. All my best jumpers have been taught by this method and I always advise any newcomer to the sport to teach their dogs to jump by the running up method.

The puppy is fitted with a collar (or choke chain) and lead and given profuse praise and titbits to induce a state of some excitement or euphoria before the first stages of this method of jumping training are attempted. When the puppy is excited by the praise afforded it, it should be run up to a low hurdle – a foot high hurdle is not too low to start the whelp – and as the trainer steps over the hurdle he jerks the lead uttering the word 'Up' or 'Over' as he does so, thereby encouraging the whelp to clear the hurdle. Effusive praise should precede and terminate every jumping training session so that the puppy actually becomes excited by the very presence of the hurdle it is required to jump. Jumping must always be a pleasurable activity to the dog and the dog should alway experience an air of excitement before it is required to jump. The very best competitive jumpers (I have mentioned the tale of Burke) are always very alert and excited when they are about to compete. Dogs which regard jumping as a chore or jump half-heartedly are seldom suitable animals for competitive jumping events, no matter how athletic the animal may be. If asked to predict the winner of a high jumping event I would certainly choose the dog that was becoming excited by the sight of other dogs attempting to clear the jumping frame, rather than a far more athletic dog that manifests an inert expression as the competition quickens.

As the training proceeds the handler must increase the height of the boards in the hurdle but continue to step over the hurdle dog on leash uttering 'Up' or 'Over' and jerking the dog's leash to encourage the animal to leap the hurdle. When the hurdle becomes too high for the handler to stride over it the handler should run the dog at the hurdle, step to the left or right of the obstruction, jerk the lead and utter the command 'Up'/'Over' as he does so. The process of exciting the lurcher by engaging it in a wild game must always precede this stage of training and if the dog refuses to jump as the handler side-steps the jumping frame (as the lurcher sometimes will) the animal should never be chastised or scolded for its failure to leap the hurdle. Rather the handler should take the dog, engage it in an exciting game once again and then while the dog is still excited, run the animal at the jumping frame again. Few excited young lurchers will refuse to jump the frame, but should the dog not jump the hurdle the exercise must finish for the day, and finish on a high note with the dog praised effusively and once again involved in an exciting game. No exercise should ever end on a sour note with an unhappy lurcher led home by a disgruntled handler.

On the subject of unhappy lurchers, nothing but nothing is guaranteed to make a lurcher puppy as unhappy as jumping it over a frame that is likely to fall and upset the dog. If this happens the dog may refuse to jump again for some time or if it is badly frightened even quit cold and never jump again. If a dog is slightly injured or merely frightened during a jumping training programme the owner should run in and engage the animal in a game. If the animal is severely injured or very distressed the lurcher owner should avoid a game at all costs until the dog has recovered sufficiently to wish to play. Merab, my best ever lurcher, was winded by a fall when she toppled a rickety gate when chasing a rabbit. She refrained from jumping for a week or so after and we retraced the training steps of her early puppyhood to give her confidence again. However not only does she fight shy of leaping the gate where she sustained the injury, but she becomes rather edgy as we approach the gate.

Competitive jumping can be great fun to the handler and the dog and at one time my interest in the activity was as near to an obsession as it was Burke's my competitive dog. Only twice did I turn up to compete but refrained from doing so and 'scratched' my dog. Both times the day of the competition was a hot one and the ground on which the dog was to compete was bone dry and iron hard. The show organisers were remiss about supplying a quantity of straw onto which the dog would land once it had leapt the hurdle and I was reluctant to see my lurcher's feet damaged and broken or badly bruised when it landed on hard ground. Both times I saw other dogs leap the obstacle and limp back to their handlers. It is policy not to jump the dog if the hurdles are rickety, badly constructed and if its landing is not buffered with deep straw, foam rubber or similar material. Both times that I withdrew the dog from competition I was ridiculed by fellow competitors but I never once regretted scratching the dog and preventing him from hurting himself. He was so willing to jump that to allow him to hurt himself seemed like a betrayal. He was not an intelligent dog, (though he had a quality akin to a sense of humour), had a fairly poor nose and was a little greyhoundy for my liking, but I never regretted including him in my strain of lurcher.

At the time of writing I am in the process of getting my saluki/greyhound bitch Canaan fit for November. She leaves Caithness to spend the winter on the Lincolnshire/Norfolk border. Caithness is short on hares, the standard quarry for a long dog of this breeding, and to date she has caught only rabbits. Alan, a friend of mine, will run the bitch throughout the winter on strong flatland hares. Alan has agreed to field the bitch for the winter but as the country he hunts is also crossed with drainage dykes Alan requires an animal that will not only hurdle fences or scale walls but leap dykes. In short, Alan requires me to teach the bitch to long jump rather than merely high jump and this too is easy to teach even a saluki/greyhound, scarcely the most biddable of long dogs.

Long jumping is so easy to teach it is amazing that some lurchers fail to leap even broad drainage ditches, and in Norfolk no dog can become a first class single-handed hare coursing dog unless it can bound across ditches and dykes. I taught Canaan, already a powerful high jumper I should add, to spring across ditches in a single day.

Two or three low hurdles are required as props to teach the puppy to long jump. Simply erect the pair of hurdles back to back and jump the dog over them. This is an easy task for a young lurcher and when the hurdles are moved a foot or so apart and the dog run up on the leash, commanded 'Up, over' as the lead is jerked, the lurcher will invariably clear both hurdles. As the hurdles are moved further and further apart the dog may start to hop one hurdle run across the intervening space and then hop the other hurdle. This action can be prevented by placing another hurdle between the first and second hurdle and, after lavishing effusive praise on the dog, leaping the animal over these hurdles. Most lurchers learn long jumping in double quick time and Canaan's speed in acquiring the skill is by no means exceptional. A strong healthy lurcher seldom finds a twelve foot leap even slightly taxing and I am certain Alan will find Canaan able to bound across any ditch or dyke she encounters during her stay in Norfolk. Her athletic ability will delight him, her remote saluki disposition may be less pleasing to him however.

6

Retrieving

It was in the early 1960s that I first encountered a non-retrieving lurcher that simply caught its quarry and stood over its catch refusing to lift the rabbit and return it to hand. At the time I believed that nature rather than nurture had produced an animal of this type, for the near demise of the rabbit when myxomatosis had appeared in Britain had produced an increase in the population of brown hares and faster, more greyhoundy lurchers were now being bred to course and catch hares rather than to be – and I reach for that much used cliche again – 'pot fillers'. It was my opinion that as lurchers became more and more saturated with sighthound blood there was a corresponding decrease in base line (blood other than sighthound) and hence a tendency to produce non-retrieving lurchers. I put my thoughts on the subject to print during those years and my work was considered, clear-sighted, a shade avant-garde perhaps, but logical. However some thirty years later I now believe I could have been quite wrong as to why so many non-retrieving lurchers appeared from the 1960s onward.

So why do lurchers fail to retrieve, and more to the point, what produced the spate of non-retrieving lurchers that began to appear after 1960? To answer these questions it might be wise to examine the Autolycus figures who kept lurchers prior to myxomatosis and to compare them to the type of person who began to field lurchers after that date.

Despite the fact that many books afford the lurcher great antiquity, there is considerable evidence to indicate that the type is of relatively recent origin. Prior to 1700 the rabbit was the 'cosseted dweller of the enclosed warren' and escapees fell foul of predators such as foxes, cats and mustelids that abounded in Britain prior to the eighteenth century. However improvements in military musketry were copied by makers of sporting guns and hence it became practicable to shoot birds on the wing. Whole estates were henceforth turned over to the rearing of gamebirds and keepers were gainfully employed to ruthlessly exterminate predators that preyed on these birds. Rabbits escaping from the enclosed warrens therefore soon established themselves in a relatively predator-free world and the superabundance of gamebirds and rabbits produced that quite unique figure the moucher, the snapper-up of unconsidered trifles and in conjunction with the moucher the lurcher evolved. The moucher, a distant relative of the deer poacher and the professional poacher (who incidentally seldom, if ever, resorted to using lurchers to achieve their goals) lived on the very edge of the law and was tolerated though seldom accepted by society. Mouchers were, by the very nature of their profession, solitary figures who worked best when alone (with dogs in tow perhaps) and did little to publicise their activities. Their loot consisted of the odd rabbit purloined from the hedgerow or unwary or wounded gamebird which the dog, which often enjoyed a strange and unique reciprocity with its owner, like as not brought to hand. Mouchers, true mouchers of the type explored and probably enjoyed by writers of the ilk of Brian Vesey Fitzgerald, seldom had a friend in tow during their jaunts and rarely kept more than one lurcher.

However, the disappearance of the rabbit in the mid-1950s caused not only a metamorphosis in the lurcher (more and more sighthound blood was added to the mixes) but produced a totally different species of lurcher owner. The new type of lurcher would have been of little use to the professional warrener, indeed after 1957 the warrener too became an endangered species – but took on the role of a knockabout poor-grade coursing greyhound or a very poor-grade long dog. The new lurcher owner looked on lurcher work as being a social event similar to a greyhound coursing meet rather than a foray to secure illicit or questionable game. Yet nothing is guaranteed to produce a non-retrieving lurcher more than the presence of other dogs on the field, dogs which will lunge at the quarry the dog is bringing to hand or, worse still, snatch at the catch the lurcher is retrieving. The majority of non-retrieving lurchers are in fact the result of training or of working a lurcher in the presence of another dog and if I have taken nearly seven hundred words to make this point I make no apology for doing so, for the majority of ruined lurchers toted around by lurcher dealers are virtually useless as retrievers simply because their early handlers worked them in conjunction with other dogs.

At the time of writing I contribute a weekly lurcher column to a sporting magazine called 'Shooting News' and I frequently receive letters or phone calls concerned with training non-retrieving lurchers to carry to hand. I have yet to receive a phone call from someone who has a lurcher puppy that has steadfastly refused to retrieve. Likewise I have yet to receive an enquiry requesting advice on retrieving training from a person who has not ruined, or is in the process of ruining, a puppy by training it to retrieve when there is another dog present. It is curious that the caller who owns a reluctant retriever is invariably aware that the presence of another dog is counter-productive to retrieving training, but invariably seeks a retrieving method that will allow the dog to retrieve game while other dogs career around and attempt to snatch the catch from the lurcher that is carrying it. There is no such method. A trainer must either train his lurcher to retrieve game without the presence of another dog in the field or room or accept a bad, intermittent or non-retrieving lurcher.

Thus the first rule of teaching a lurcher to retrieve is to clear the decks of other dogs, children or inquisitive adults before even attempting to teach the first steps of the retrieving training programme to the lurcher puppy. A quiet place sans dogs, sans children, sans nosey people, sans all, is the ideal place to teach retrieving training, is in fact the only place to teach retrieving.

Retrieving is simplicity itself to teach a puppy providing, that is, the owner is not short on commonsense, for dogs of all breeds are all too easily ruined by mishandling and thoughtless retrieving training. There are however two methods of teaching a dog to retrieve, fun retrieving and force retrieving, both of which will be explained presently, but the essence of all retrieving training, indeed of all dog training, is commonsense and the trainer's ability to be able to sense when to push and when to pull, so to speak, or to adapt general training programmes to the needs of a particular dog.

As a general rule, a healthy puppy will take to basic retrieving training like a duck to water and as soon as a puppy has arrived and settled into my home I start teaching the whelp to retrieve. As to the best place to start a lurcher whelp retrieving, I find a long passageway, blind-ended, with no obstructions or furniture under which the whelp can crawl, nearly impossible to beat. I avoid a crowded room, a spot cluttered with furniture or an open field like the plague when I first start teaching retrieving training.

I start training with a rolled up ball of paper – a crinkled reject sheet of typescript or a glossy magazine cover is ideal – for the nature of the material ensures the ball makes a slight noise when it is being thrown. I usually sit on the floor of the passageway and gently roll the ball of paper with my hands, ignoring the puppy and behaving as if the ball was a treasured possession. If the puppy tries to mouth the ball I lift the paper ball and behave as if I really wish to possess the object. When the puppy is thoroughly curious about the object I am coveting, I roll the ball to some four feet from me and invariably the sight of a rolling object and the sound the paper ball makes while it is rolling will cause the puppy to chase after and probably mouth and pick up the ball. I then immediately place my face at a level with that of the puppy and call the animal to me with a gentle placatory tone to my voice (this is no time for the 'Fetch it, sir!' tone of voice, for a puppy is easily vexed or cowed by such a tone). The puppy will either return to hand carrying the paper ball with it or drop the ball and race to the handler to be petted. If the puppy brings the ball to hand I gently ease the object from its mouth, uttering profuse praise while I do so, and prepare to roll the ball again. If the whelp returns to hand without the ball I still praise the animal (after all it has returned to hand) and rise and fetch the paper ball and prepare to throw it again. Sooner or later most puppies, even pure bred Middle Eastern sighthounds, will pick up and attempt to carry the paper ball and owner, face to the floor, will seldom need to pretend to be pleased with the whelp's performance.

Some whelps, as few as one in a hundred I should add, will show little interest in chasing the paper ball and now the trainer must rack his brains to find a method which will encourage the whelp not only to run forward but also actually pick up the dummy. When I have encountered a lurcher puppy that has shown a natural disinclination to mouth and pick up the dummy I adopt a method that harnesses the whelp's desire to chase rather than accept its disinclination to retrieve. I attach the ball to a length of twine and tow the ball in front of the whelp. I have yet to see a lurcher puppy that would not chase this 'cat and mouse' device, and while many will attempt to trap the elusive ball with their feet (it is said that both collie crosses and salukis alike will usually try to catch their first game with their feet), it is only a matter of time before the lurcher puppy grabs the 'mouse' with its mouth. The trainer, still holding the string attached to the mouse, should gently tow the rope to animate the mouse but take great care not to hurt or frighten the whelp while doing so. The trainer must then gently ease the mouse from the puppy's mouth and resume the game. When the puppy snatches at the mouse, as soon as it appears the paper ball plus string can be thrown and the lurcher whelp will usually rush to and pick up the mouse while the trainer lowers his face to the level of the puppy's and calls the whelp to hand. Praise, and lavish praise is really important to reinforce the training pattern, and the owner will probably look extremely foolish to the observer (who is probably not dog-orientated anyway) as he cavorts and praises the puppy.

If the lurcher enthusiast is afraid to rupture his image by giving effusive praise to his whelp or speaking in tones that resemble baby talk to the puppy that has succeeded in performing a task it would be wise for the owner to forget training a puppy and join the host that enjoy parading large deerhoundy animals around a showring and inviting the judge to choose which lurcher is the prettiest. A dog trainer attempting to train a puppy must accept the fact he will seldom seem dignified while training his whelp and if a masculine image is all important it would be wise for such a person to forget dog training. It has been suggested that the reason why women succeed so well as obedience trainers is that women have no machismo image to lose.

I normally continue training in the passageway for another week or so until the puppy comes to hand instantly. In such a passage the whelp has no place to carry his treasure and chew it and no furniture under which it can hide to engage in its game with the dummy or mouse. The fewer recesses or hiding places a dog training ground has the easier it will be to call the whelp to hand. Once the whelp has thoroughly mastered the technique of picking up the dummy and carrying it to hand, each and every time it is thrown, it is time to change both location and dummy.

One moment though before passing onto the next portion of the training programme. The handler must always be careful never to sicken the puppy by expecting the whelp to fetch the dummy too often. A sad, dispirited or bored expression on the puppy's face is the canine equivalent of an oil light going on on the dashboard of a car – the trainer/driver has driven the puppy/vehicle a shade too far! The trainer must always quit while the puppy is still enjoying the game of fetching to hand and the puppy should be so enthused by the game that it will literally beg the owner to continue the training session. If the trainer throws the dummy just one too many times the training programme has taken ten backward steps. If I once observe a puppy appearing bored I promptly hide the dummy, take out the 'cat and mouse' string and paper and engage the puppy in a game of chasing and catching, and I allow the puppy to catch and play with the mouse. It is sound advice to end every training session with a game of some sort and the best game in which to involve a lurcher puppy that has begun to sour of a retrieving session is 'cat and mouse'. Puppies must always be wildly excited at the end of every training session of any sort – even if the trainer has to deliberately and artificially induce this excitement in his whelp. Training must always be fun for the dog.

Most of the letters I receive from 'Shooting News' concern problems regarding the second stage of retrieving training that I shall describe presently. Once the puppy retrieves relatively proficiently in the passageway it is time to move to a room in the house or the backyard or garden to continue the training. Expect squalls when one trains outside the house for the first time. Any garden, or backyard for that matter, must exude a host of strange smells that will excite a puppy and command its attention. Allow the whelp to explore and to savour such scents for some time before attempting to interest the whelp in the dummy you expect the puppy to retrieve, for it is a racing certainty the puppy will find such scents more interesting than the dummy you are about to throw. It is far, far worse when the trainer ventures into a park in which several dogs have been allowed to romp, urinate and defecate, for such uriniferous waste and faecal matter, while it must appear disgusting to the human nose, will be terrifically exciting to canine nostrils. At the time of writing dog trainers are making big business out of training recalcitrant dogs that are kept by owners in large cities and train both dog and owner in large parks. It requires terrific knowledge of canine behaviour to control a dog in this environment and henceforth I will digress somewhat to mention what to do if one trains a dog under these conditions and the dog breaks training, 'cuts and runs', engages in a wild caper with another dog and, sin of sins, refuses to come to hand when called. The trainer, retrieving dummy in his hand, is left looking extremely foolish when the puppy careers around and refuses to return, despite the fact that the trainer cajoles, coaxes and finally rants and storms while the puppy races around like a dog possessed. Sooner or later any puppy will encounter a situation which prompts it to behave in this manner and the whelp promptly the most destructive practice a trainer can ever devise. Dogs must always feel a sensation of pleasure when their names are uttered, which is basically why a dog decides to come to hand to its name; it expects reward either in the form of petting or food. At the time of writing it is unfashionable to train a dog by rewarding it with titbits. However, fashionable or not, if a lurcher (scarcely the easiest dog to train) responds to titbits during its training programme then by all means use food as a vehicle for training. My own lurchers run in my yard, or on the moor near the house, and each time I venture out of doors I call them by name and reward them by praise or food when they come to hand. I hasten to add that some of my lurchers are over twenty years of age, yet are still rewarded when they come to hand. If the trainer devises a method of training a particular dog to come instantly to hand he should disregard fashionable ideas of dog training and stick to that method. My own dogs are, partly by dint of their nature and partly because of my methods of training, a little too effusive in the way they react when they meet me, but they return instantly to hand whenever their names are uttered.

Lead training must follow hot on heels of recall training and straight away I must admit that I dislike lead training for it distresses both the puppy and, I confess, me. Were it not for my insufferable pride I would, I admit, allow others to lead train my puppies. Nevertheless I steel myself and set aside one day of the puppy's initial training programme for basic lead training and endeavour to reduce the trauma a puppy is bound to experience when its movements are restricted by the lead for the very first time in its short life. Some greyhound trainers have a series of methods that are designed to reduce the trauma of lead training a large batch of puppies. A collar is attached to the neck of the whelp and the puppy is returned to its litter mates. For an hour or two the puppy will scratch at the collar and attempt to remove the encumbrance but in a matter of a day the puppy will readily accept the presence of a collar around its neck. After a day or so, a lead or a clip with a length of rope is attached to the collar around the puppy's neck, and the whelp is returned to its litter mates. The whelp will tow around the rope for a few days with its litter mates snatching at the rope or lead, and sooner or later – two days is usually enough – the whelp will usually be ready for conventional lead training. This is rather an antique method of lead training perhaps, but it is still practised in large kennels of gundogs and greyhound kennels in Britain and America. It is however a method that is thwart with danger. Puppies strangle to death all too easily when the line becomes tangled on an obstruction, so the kennel man who uses this method must forever keep a weather eye open for squalls when using this means of lead training.

I would certainly fight shy of the once popular method of breaking a whelp or foal to the lead. This method which consists of simply tying up a horse or sapling hound with head or neck attachments to a rope and leaving the animal to its own devices in a barn is traumatic to say the very least and extremely perilous to the animal being trained by this method. Hancock in his 1989 diary tells the tale of a traveller who came to his kennel looking for 'a deal', an expression that would make me extremely wary of the potential client, I must add. Hancock sold the man an inoculated sapling for the same price as a puppy but warned the traveller the whelp was shy of the lead. Hancock was, however, assured that the traveller knew exactly how to lead break the dog. A few days later the man returned to complain that he had tied up the sapling to a pile of scrap iron and the animal had strangled itself. After reading this extract of the Hancock diary, it reinforced my desire to avoid the method and my resolve to vet every person who obtained a puppy from me even more carefully than I had previously done.

Sooner or later the puppy will need to be placed on a collar or choke chain and then lead trained. When a puppy is first fitted with a lead it will display one of two reactions to the lead, it will either fight or flop and forthwith I must say that I find the fighter infinitely easier to train than the flopper. A fighter will buck, roll, throw itself around, and often seize the leash or chain in its mouth to escape the lead. The flopper will fall on its belly or back and refuse to move, a look of either horror or utter dejection on its face – a look that leaves the trainer scratching his head as to what to do next.

A fighter is easily lead trained and should be allowed to play out its original panic during which time it will almost certainly attempt by dint of its struggles to wrap itself around its owner's legs. The owner has but to turn with the puppy to prevent the tangle and the process also helps allow the puppy to accept the restrictions imposed on it by the lead. When the fighter has played out its initial resentment for the restriction imposed on it by the lead it will usually walk sulkily on the lead, racing ahead occasionally and even bucking and rearing to be free of its leash, but if the owner is careful and does not become angry or upset by the action of the whelp, then in days the animal will no longer dread the appearance of the lead and accept the restrictions the lead imposes sheds all the training restraint and control with which the trainer has indoctrinated the puppy and literally runs wild.

The tyro trainer cannot be blamed if he coaxes, wheedles awhile maybe, before raving and storming and resorts to finally chasing the recalcitrant whelp and then, sin of sins, thrashes the youngster. Reader, I have made these mistakes and now realise the error of my ways, so I bid you take notice and heed the advice of one who has erred.

Once a puppy cuts and runs, or worse still, encounters a dog of a like age, it will almost certainly run riot and (this is true of the most highly trained young whelp) there is not the slightest thing a trainer can do about it until the puppy has run off its initial enthusiasm for the caper in which it is indulging. At best the trainer can salvage some of his pride and act in a nonchalant way as if he intended the puppy to exercise in such a manner. It is futile to call, to shout, to scream, and what is more, if the trainer is able to chase after and catch a lurcher puppy what he needs is not a lurcher but an Olympic Games selection panel, for the trainer will also be fast enough to catch a rabbit without the use of a dog and hence will be able to leave Carl Lewis standing at the blocks so to speak.

The trainer should sit or stand awhile, uttering not a word while the puppy runs itself into a state of near exhaustion and then, as it begins to lose enthusiasm for the game, the handler should pretend to ignore the whelp and walk away. The chances are the whelp will follow. If it doesn't, keep an eye on the puppy until it is clearly fed up with the game and then encourage it to follow the handler. When it does, greet it like a long lost friend, biting one's lips to stifle back one's fury perhaps, and engage the whelp in a game before leashing it up and taking it home. Under no circumstances display displeasure/temper/fury when the whelp comes to hand, although this is often more easily said than done. As sure as the sun will rise tomorrow, sooner or later the lurcher trainer with a puppy in tow will experience such problems when he endeavours to train a dog in a place where other dogs or children frequent. If the puppy runs after children or adults it is virtually useless to ask people not to play with the puppy and hence encourage it to follow them and the trainer is best employed getting children and adults to hold the puppy until it can be placed back on its leash again. Training a dog in a public place is a practice fraught with difficulties and one I personally avoid like the plague.

The puppy must continue with its retrieving training programme long after it has mastered the technique of fetching the dummy it has been commanded to retrieve instantly and without question. At some point in the training programme the trainer is likely to encounter his second problem, for lurchers usually become bored easily and once they have soured of retrieving it is difficult to rekindle an interest in the activity again. Every measure should be taken to stop the dog souring of retrieving and one of the best ways of doing this is to change the dummy as often as possible. The crinkly paper ball will keep a whelp interested for a brief spell, after which a toilet roll cardboard centre can be used as a dummy; this can be replaced with a ball or an old slipper (puppies are often enthusiastic about fetching evil-smelling objects to hand). Sooner or later the whelp will sour of retrieving even the most pungent slipper and this may be substituted for a dried rabbit skin dummy. When interest in retrieving a dried rabbit skin diminishes the dummy can be given a short reprieve by animating the object with a cat and mouse line before throwing it and requesting the puppy to bring the dummy to hand.

Eventually the puppy will begin to sicken of the act of retrieving the dried rabbit skin dummy and the trainer may decide to resort to using a dead rabbit as a training aid and now the tyro trainer may experience a shock – a surprise that often makes the newcomer to the art of lurcher training lose interest in the training project and sell his puppy. Many, many lurchers are terrified when they first encounter their first rabbit cadaver. Please do not write the puppy off as a failure because he seems afraid of the dead rabbit. Under no circumstances consider that the animal will not chase live rabbits because it displays a fear of a rabbit cadaver. One of my present lurchers, an excellent and very game bitch I call Phaedra, ran off and refused to approach me when she saw her first dead rabbit and was requested to retrieve the object. If the puppy is frightened by the cadaver ignore the whelp and animate the cadaver with a cat and mouse string (neighbours watching the trainer towing a dead rabbit around the garden may well consider the handler to be demented, so this aspect of training must certainly be conducted in private). It is almost a certainty that the puppy will come to investigate the carcase that is now moving around the training area. In no time at all the puppy will begin mouthing the object and carrying the carcase around in its mouth and from this time forth many lurchers become shy of retrieving a conventional dummy.

Once the lurcher has started carrying a rabbit carcase to hand the most destructive event that can occur is for another dog to appear on the scene, for a natural retriever is invariably a jealous retriever (I shall explain this presently) and a great deal of damage can be done if the other dog snatches at the carcase the lurcher is carrying to hand. Only once have I trained a lurcher/long dog that was indifferent to the presence of another dog when it was retrieving a cadaver or live rabbit to hand. My present long dog, a saluki/greyhound hybrid I call Canaan, is stupid, recalcitrant and prone to erratic behaviour, however she carries to hand when even a crowd of other dogs is in the hunting field. Merab, the most intelligent lurcher I have ever owned, is however very shy of fetching to hand if another dog is near me.

Mob-handed hunters, lurcher enthusiasts who seem unwilling to venture forth alone without the company of a dozen or so other lurcher enthusiasts and their dogs, seldom own well-trained lurchers, yet seem totally content with the bedlam that would cause embarrassment to any thinking lurchermen. Hunting a lurcher in conjunction with another dog of any breed is bad practice. A good, well-trained lurcher should enjoy a one man relationship with its owner – other dogs no matter how well-trained they may be inspire a good retrieving lurcher to become jealous with its catch and shy of retrieving its catch to hand.

However, some dogs will not retrieve by conventional training methods, though I have yet to encounter a puppy that could not be trained to retrieve by the methods just advised. However, such is the state of much handled, much sold, badly mentally damaged, totally untrained lurchers that are the stock in trade of dog dealers that it becomes expedient to mention that most controversial of subjects, force retrieving training, which is not (or rather should not be) what the name implies. The reader must now either miss a page or so or steel himself to read of the technique known as force retrieving training or, less accurately perhaps, what shortly after World War I was known as the German Method of retrieving training.

Force training simply consists of persuading, (sometimes a delightful euphemism for what was often to follow), the dog to open its mouth and seize the dummy between its jaws and, barbaric as such training may sound (and often used to be), it is an extremely successful method of teaching a reluctant retriever to fetch to hand. The German method in its purest form is a terrifying way of teaching the family pet to retrieve and relies on the fact that dogs are pure hedonists – they enjoy pleasure and will literally do anything to avoid pain. Konrad Most in his book 'Dog Training' was one of the first to describe force training methods, but such methods had been used both on the Continent and in Britain decades before Most's birth. Basically, the dog about to be trained was fitted with a spiked collar, the tines or spikes of which pointed inwards, and when the collar was properly fitted, just touched the delicate skin of the dog's neck and throat. When the dog was deemed ready, if any dog is ready for what was to follow, the collar was twisted so that the tines bit into the dog's neck and throat and, not surprisingly, the dog opened its jaws either to bite at its assailant or to gasp in agony. As it did so the dumb-bell was thrust with almost surgical skill into the dog's mouth so that the bar of the dumb-bell touched the lips at the back of the dog's mouth. Immediately the bar touched, the trainer uttered the word 'Hold' or 'Fetch' and at the same instant released the collar. Thus the dog, admittedly over a fairly long period of time, came to associate the relief from fearsome pain with fetching an object it had been sent to retrieve. I have deliberately over-simplified the process simply because such methods are illegal in Britain but also because this type of force training method is unsuitable for training sighthounds, which often suffer dreadfully from such training methods.

Basically, if one strips the next process to the barest of bones, it differs little from the technique just described and also relies on the dog's hedonistic tendencies equally as much as the system described by Konrad Most. However, this method is a perfectly legal one to use in any part of Great Britain.

The handler first collars and leads the dog to prevent the animal running away if it finds the training programme distasteful, and few dogs enjoy a force training session of any sort, one should add. So to the business of simple force training. Firstly, no lurcher enthusiast should attempt to train a dog that not only has acquired a certain degree of obedience training but also a degree of trust in the handler, for the training session that is to follow must at first seem little short of bewildering to the dog.

The owner/handler should place the dog at the sit position and by dint of passing the hand over the dog's muzzle and pressing the dog's lips against its gums and teeth cause the animal to open its mouth. Once the animal has opened its mouth the dumb-bell is thrust into the dog's mouth and the command 'Fetch' is uttered. It is essential that the dog is made to hold the dumb-bell and not spit it out as if the equipment was covered with a foul-tasting substance or drop the object as if the dog believes the handler has suddenly become deranged. Some dogs will display an emotion akin to terror when the trainer resorts to this method of training, but it is essential, particularly on that first training session, that the owner/handler ensures that the dog continues to hold the dumb-bell.

When the dog finally holds the dumb-bell in its mouth, no matter how bewildered its expression may be, I heap praise upon the dog as if I believe the dog has performed some wonderous feat by simply holding the dumb-bell in its mouth. I then take the dumb-bell from the dog's mouth uttering 'Give' or something similar although I stick to the same commands when training any dog. However, I never allow the dog to drop the dumb-bell when it decides to do so. I then repeat the exercise two or three times but no more and with luck the dog starts to believe that I am perhaps less a lunatic than I appeared a few seconds ago.

At first it is perhaps good sense to restrict these holding sessions to a few seconds and then as both dog and trainer gain confidence in this training technique the dog should be made to hold the dumb-bell for a considerable period of time, but the handler must still give effusive praise to the dog before and after it completes each stage of the exercise. When the dog does finally open its mouth in anticipation of the dumb-bell being placed between its jaws the handler will not need to feign pleasure. Indeed he may well find he has to restrain himself from over-praising the dog. My first sighthound trained by the German Method was an imported saluki I attempted to teach to retrieve. For a while I confess I made a complete pig's ear out of the method and it was often hard to conceal my exasperation when I found I had made little or no progress throughout the day. Quite suddenly the whole training programme seemed to gel and for a while I felt an elation I have seldom experienced in my life. The dog opened his mouth, accepted the dumb-bell and held it between his jaws as soon as I uttered the word 'Fetch'. However I failed dismally in my efforts to get the dog to seize the dumb-bell when it was held in front of him. One day when all seemed lost and the fabric of my own private little world seemed rather shaky, to say the least, he began to lick the dumb-bell and the next day he reached out and took the dumb-bell in his jaws.

He had been my thoughts in waking and sleeping for six weeks and my triumphs and disasters in his training were reflected in my high and low moods during the weeks. I had never experienced any success in the training of a saluki, but I set-to training this one with such determination I was virtually bound to succeed, though I became the classic bore relating my training successes to friends who had absolutely no interest in dog training.

As I moved the dumb-bell further and further from his lips he would reach out and stretch his elegant neck in order to seize the dumb-bell as soon as I uttered the command 'Fetch', but his actions were slow and deliberate, as is the way with Middle Eastern sighthounds, and his training progressed with an infuriating slowness. However when I dropped the dumb-bell a few yards from his nose, he seemed bewildered as to what to do when I uttered the command 'Fetch'. He simply did not associate mouthing the dumb-bell when he was stationed at any position other than sit. When the dumb-bell was brought to him he could, by dint of craning his neck, mouth the dumb-bell and understood exactly what to do. However, once the dumb-bell fell to the floor and he needed to break the sit to fetch the object he simply could not understand how to make the next step in the training programme. I have related the curious tale of how I learnt the secrets to teach the hound in 'Commonsense Dog Training' and it is sufficient to say that by pushing the dog's head in a rhythmic fashion towards the object, he eventually rose, mouthed and carried the dummy. He progressed slowly in his training and finally he would walk out and bring to hand any object I left as much as a hundred yards away. He continued to retrieve long after he was returned to his owner and for many years I was sent a Christmas card that was made from a photograph of a dog carrying some dummy to hand. I savour this tale, it is my one and only success in training salukis to any standard I considered to be fairly obedient.

Force training, the German Method (how derogatory and xenophobic are the British, each unpleasant human characteristic is said to be the malaise of foreigners, Dutch courage, Irish wisdom etc.), may appear to be a complete bore and totally time consuming, as indeed it often is, yet most professional dog trainers swear by this method and even force train dogs that show a natural inclination to retrieve. It is argued that a force trained dog will always fetch the object it has been sent to retrieve but a fun trained dog will sometimes decide it is not in the mood to fulfil the command and no amount of coaxing will persuade it to do so. Whatever the logic of such statements and there is neither time nor space to debate the logic in a book of this kind, most professional trainers and police-dog handlers will adopt the German Method to train their dogs even if the dog shows a natural propensity to carry to hand.

Even if the lurcher is force trained and fielded by itself and never in the company of another dog there are times when it may well display certain peculiarities that the lurcherman must endeavour to correct. Some lurchers, seldom lurchers that have been force trained one should add, will return their catch to hand yet refuse to give up their catches and hold them in a vice-like grip, others will drop their catches and allow them to run off. However, the most infuriating creature is the dog that comes almost to hand then, rabbit in mouth, steadfastly refuses to come to the owner and give up its catch. Once the dog manifests the slightest peculiarity in retrieving, the owner/handler should sit down and think out why a certain peculiarity has begun to manifest itself and if possible take the puppy back over the same training programme to correct the fault.

Young dogs will sometimes carry to hand yet refuse to release the object, gripping them even more tightly when the handler reaches for the dummy the dog is carrying. The handler must now persuade the dog to release its catch and the best way to do this is for the trainer to place a hand over the dog's muzzle and gently (and 'gently' is indeed the operative word) squeeze the dog's lips against its teeth. If this is done properly the dog will usually relax its grip on the object and yield up the dummy to the handler. However excessive pressure or another activity that actually hurts the dog usually has the effect of producing an animal that is reluctant to return its catch to hand. The dog that does not bring its dummy directly to hand but drops the catch some feet from the handler is an embryonic nuisance and will lose many of the rabbits it has caught. Once the dog fetches live rabbits almost to hand and drops them, those rabbits will attempt to escape and if they have not been damaged by the dog often will succeed in finding sanctuary before the dog can catch them a second time. I find that if the dog drops a dummy a few yards from the handler, the handler can rectify this fault by turning his back and walking away from the dog which is still holding the dummy. I then turn and take the dummy from the dog's mouth and praise and reward the dog for its return to hand. I have yet to find this technique to fail to teach a dog to carry to hand though I have had many dogs that retrieved first of the season catches to hand and released the rabbits only to catch them again and never during the same season made the same mistake a second time.

Circlers, dogs that return almost to hand with rabbit or dummy in mouth and then begin to circle the handler with their catch, moving just out of reach as the handler moves to take the catch or dummy from the dog, set my teeth on edge. My anger, however, is not directed at the poor, misguided lurcher, jealously carrying its catch or dummy, but at the person who trained the dog. Circlers are made, not born. They are a product of nurture, not nature. They are created by bad training methods and are seldom, if ever, innately reluctant to yield up their catches. Every circler I have ever been asked to retrain developed the habit because the handler insisted on having another dog present when the dog fetched its catch to hand.

Lamping parties, bands of youths, or men who are old enough to know better, who venture out with two or more dogs on slips, are very productive at producing dogs that will show a tendency to circle. It is a maddening habit and I cringe when I see a lurcher party out for a day's coursing or a band of lampers, half a dozen dogs on slips, bound for a foray. Nothing can be more destructive to training methods. Nothing can ruin an otherwise eager retriever.

My own strain of lurcher, and I use the word 'strain' correctly, for the family now breed true enough to be classed as a strain, are potentially the worst circlers imaginable. The collie blood allows them to form a tight bond with the handler and the lurchers need the one-to-one relationship that old-fashioned lurchers once enjoyed with the mouchers who owned them. However, despite the fact that the family are natural retrievers and invariably carry to hand with virtually little or no training, they are the worst retrievers if they find another dog present when they attempt to return their catches to hand. Hence I take some pains to advise anyone who has one of the strain, to work the puppy separately far from the company of other dogs.

Of all the lurchers I have seen in my life my own strain are the most deeply jealous retrievers and at one time I believed that some facet of my own desire to hunt alone had somehow found it way into the genetic make up of the dog – highly unscientific thinking by any standards perhaps. I now realise the reason I am a solitary person is that I've witnessed the bedlam of lamping and coursing parties so often that I've learned to shed unnecessary companions and superfluous dogs when I hunt my lurchers.

Peculiarities concerning retrieving techniques will sometimes correct themselves but more often than not they will need to be ironed out by a careful retraining programme.

7

Stock-breaking

The sight of a lurcher hunting along a hedgerow or coursing a hare is usually enough to cause apoplexy in any stock-keeper, particularly the sheep farmer. Lurchers usually have a terrific hunting instinct and when badly trained become amongst the very worst stock worriers imaginable. I cannot resist repeating the incredible tale of the Beast of Watten to illustrate my point the better. Watten is a tiny village in Caithness, having a districtual population of less than three or four hundred people perhaps, for the district is rich in sheep and store cattle. Some years ago a crofter reported the loss of a sheep to a police officer in the village. While stock worrying is not unknown in the district where collies (amongst the worst stock worriers is a collie turned rogue) abound, little more was thought of the incident until a spate of stock worrying occurred. Whole flocks of sheep were driven against the sheep fence and ripped and torn as though a fiend of some sort had set about them. The incident coincided with the appearance of a huge black cat (a possible hybrid between the Scottish wild cat and the domesticated or feral cats, so zoologists believe) that appeared in Brora, a district some fifty miles further south. However, when young calves were added to the toll of victims torn and mangled by the creature it just was such that a host of newspaper reporters journeyed north to obtain a rather sensational scoop. For some reason the slaughter stopped as soon as the press arrived and sceptics were prepared to accept the beast as a northerly edition of the Loch Ness Monster, a creature that becomes active during the tourist season but experiences a curious absence whenever a scientific investigator appears. The press began to laugh off the incident and prepared to go home to rather angry, expense-counting editors when the killing began again and small flocks of sheep were mutilated and slain. A huge hunting party of beaters, gunmen and farmers was formed and the group was aided by a police helicopter carrying a skilled marksman. The drive roused a huge fawn lurcher that sprang from the lodgepole pine plantations and was brought down by a helicopter-based marksman. The killing stopped abruptly but, not surprisingly, Caithness is decidedly anti-lurcher these days.

However lurchers are so easily stock-broken that it is a wonder that so many lurcher enthusiasts who supposedly hunt their dogs regularly have lurchers that are unsteady with sheep. A sheep-chaser, or even a lurcher that pays too much attention to sheep, is an absolute pest. Its mind is seldom totally on the job in hand and when such a dog disappears over a rise after legitimate quarry the animal causes such anxiety that a pleasurable day takes on the nature of a nightmare.

I make a point of walking a six-week-old puppy I am considering training among sheep so that the dog associates the presence of sheep with a feeling akin to trepidation rather than pleasure. I also add that should a dog pursue sheep and gain pleasure from the experience other than by dint of the fact that the sheep are running from the whelp, or worse still, by the fact that the whelp has managed to bite the fleeing sheep, henceforth the animal becomes the very devil to break from sheep worrying.

Most, in his book *Dog Training*, is of the opinion that the dog is basically a cowardly creature (cowardice and courage are often misunderstood qualities when a person attempts to attribute them to animals, one should add) and that if an animal decides to face down a dog, the dog is unlikely to wish to take the attack to that animal (there is actually a far more likely explanation for this behaviour). However should an animal decide to flee when a dog appears, it literally invites the dog to attack and kill the frightened creature. Hence breeds of sheep that are naturally fearful of dogs are not only more likely to be attacked by dogs, but are the very worst breeds of sheep to which a dog can be introduced. Sheep which stand their ground are certainly the best sheep to use for breaking a puppy of the tendency to worry sheep. Shetland rams, small primitive sheep that are often as unafraid of men as they are of dogs, are ideal and will terrify a puppy by their presence. I suppose I am extremely fortunate in as much as while I am surrounded by northern Cheviot sheep, paranoid and fearful creatures, I have access to black-faced rams that are bold enough to view a dog with disdain. Phaedra, one of my lurcher bitches, was not stock-broken until she was six months of age – I had been ill for several months after her birth – but needed to be restrained with a checkline to prevent her from running away when she first encountered one of these rams.

Sheep will seldom flee before a six-week-old whelp, however, and hence the very young whelp should be introduced to sheep as soon as it is broken to the lead. If the whelp pulls the leash and attempts to play with the sheep the line or leash should be jerked sharply and the word 'No' uttered in a sharp and frightening tone. Two or three days of such training will usually subdue even the most determined whelp from chasing sheep.

There is a problem regarding breaking lurchers to stock or of training lurchers generally that is seldom mentioned yet is very, very real. Most lurcher owners come by their dogs second or third hand after the animals have been mistrained, untrained, misused and abused by others. Many lurcher owners come by dogs that are confirmed stock worriers, dogs which have pulled down and killed sheep on forays into the countryside. Indeed there have been instances of lurcher owners deliberately using their dogs to seek out and kill sheep, and stock-keepers have been dismayed to find the viscera of lambs on bloodied pasture (small wonder farmers are antipathetic towards lurcher owners generally). To break habitual stock worriers or dogs which display a natural propensity to chase and harm sheep is, however, quite a problem.

Modern practice tends to be to watch the dog's attitude towards sheep while the owner keeps the dog on a check leash. If the dog displays an interest or animosity towards sheep (displays pleasure or interest in pursuing sheep), then at the moment the dog lunges forward a sharp noise or unpleasant sensation should replace the pleasure the dog has felt when it attempted to chase the sheep. Some trainers advocate jerking a check-line sharply as the dog lunges forward and either banging a loud gong or firing a particularly noisy starting pistol to frighten the dog. This action can however be counter-productive for the loud noise may also frighten the sheep and the sight of sheep fleeing before the dog may excite the lurcher further. Modern methods of replacing pleasure with pain to iron out emotional and behavioural problems do, in fact, work better in a laboratory than they do in the field. I find taking the dog on a leash amongst bunched sheep and jerking the lead or phyically chastising the dog if it displays an unhealthy interest in the sheep, let alone attempts to chase or attack them, just as, if not more, effective.

A tried, tested and certainly efficacious method of breaking a dog to sheep that might well invite prosecution is the act of chaining a dog to a ram with a six or seven feet length of line. I hasten to add that this method should never be used on a dog that has shown no indication it wishes to worry sheep, or used to break a puppy to sheep. Once again, any ram, or aggressive ewe for that matter, may be used but black-faced tups (particularly cadereared imprints) or Shetland rams are certainly the most efficacious at convincing a dog that it is folly to worry sheep, or more to the point, this particular sheep; and this point is more important than the majority of trainers realise, but I'll explain this statement later.

In principle, the dog is tied to a rather aggressive sheep and once it realises the sheep is a potential victim, it attacks the ram. The ram, particularly if the ram is an imprint, seldom waits to be attacked and charges, head down, to meet the aggressor. The boss of a sheep's skull is virtually impregnable to the bite of even a pit bull terrier and when this mass of bone and horn, propelled by up to two hundred pounds of muscle, strikes a dog it is a very strong and powerful lurcher that is still standing after such a charge. The dog rises and either attacks the sheep whereupon it receives yet another trouncing or attempts to flee but by doing so pulls the ram towards it, thereby inviting another attack. The sheep, particularly if it has been used to break difficult dogs before, will now usually stand stockstill and face down the dog awaiting its next move, and this waiting period is usually as terrifying to the dog as the blow from the horn and bone. This training method will either make the dog wary of attacking this particular sheep or any sheep (and I have seen dogs that shun certain rams but will still worry other sheep) – dogs are often more perspicuous than people imagine. Conversely, it is possible that a dog so treated may well develop an implacable hatred of sheep for the rest of its days and may attack them on sight. My own strain of lurcher – and Phaedra, one of my bitches, had an inbuilt fear of sheep for some reason or other – would be demoralised by the first charge of the sheep. But I have encountered lurchers particularly some of the pit bull terrier hybrids that are now quite popular, but illegal to produce one should add, that would react quite furiously if battered and broken by a ram.

More to the point I am not absolutely certain if such training methods don't constitute criminal offences. I've seen dogs terribly injured by rams to which they have been tethered and, likewise, I've seen rams finish up with lacerated ears when the dog had the temerity to retaliate against the pounding head and horns of the ram. I'm not certain if an observer who was antipathetic to any form of cruelty might be successful if he or she brought a private action against someone they observed tethering a dog to a ram for the purposes just described. It is certainly an offence under Section 1, 1A of the Protection of Animals Act 1911 to 'cause an animal unnecessary suffering by wantonly or unreasonably doing, or omitting to do any act'.

Whether the battering given the dog by the ram constitutes unnecessary suffering would be debatable perhaps. Nevertheless, many psychologists who are engaged in modifying unacceptable canine behaviour resort to the use of truckling sheep to discipline dogs. Mugford, 'Dr. Mugford's Casebook', shows a ram facing down a hostile dog and this training method is practised by shepherds the world over.

A dog about to be broken to livestock of any sort should be encouraged to feel a sense of isolation to deflate its confidence. Hence it is very bad policy to attempt to stock-break two or more puppies at the same time. One puppy will feel desperately alone when faced by an aggressive ram or a somewhat prickly gamefowl, but two or more puppies will gain courage by the presence of litter mates or friends and what should be a morale-deflating exercise can all too easily turn into a wild game which has the effect of encouraging rather than discouraging the whelps from attacking stock.

On the subject of breaking dogs to stock it would be virtually impossible to leave the subject without mentioning the notions of the late Barbara Woodhouse and her suggestions concerning breaking chicken-killing dogs in her book 'Training Dogs My Way', and the outrage these suggestions caused amongst the dog owning fraternity. Mrs. Woodhouse advocated taking the dog to a chicken pen, leashing the dog with a correctly fitted choke chain, suddenly chopping off a chicken's head and allowing the torso of the bird to flap around the yard while the dog attempted to attack the carcase from which blood in copious amounts would flow. The dog would have its chain jerked to intimidate or frighten it (and one supposed that the chicken would also feel a shade less than happy about the experience) and in theory the dog would be broken of its habits. Shades of the macabre perhaps yet such a method would not contravene any aspect of the 1911 Protection of Animals Act, though it would certainly offend human decency. At the risk of lampooning O. Henry (one of my favourite writers), 'I never yet see'd a woman who was good with horses that wasn't hell on fowl', and let's leave the method to those who enjoy such capers. I have never used this method – nor would I.

If asked to break dogs to poultry I would simply apply the same basic principles I have used to break the dog to sheep: to the chicken pen, jerking the lead, uttering 'No' in a sharp tone and repeating this action day in, day out, for a month or so to break the animal of its propensity to kill fowl. I think I'd stop short at decapitating a fowl but I'm probably a softy. My own strain of lurchers have a natural propensity to carry live fowl – and I have to break my puppies of this habit as soon as they are able to be lead trained. I seldom breed a lurcher that is really troublesome with chickens, possibly because I keep fowl and my lurchers see them every day.

Ducks are very inviting for lurchers to attack and kill – they are in fact the perfect prey for any dog – they are timid, totally inoffensive, panic easily and are noisy when terrified. Most untrained lurchers find them little short of irresistible and need careful breaking to ensure they leave ducks strictly alone. Yet lurchers that are totally steady with Khaki Campbells, ducks I keep, still bring down mallards and widgeon – despite the fact that the Khaki Campbell was originally bred from a wild mallard drake.

The whole knack of breaking a lurcher to poultry of any sort is for either the handler to keep poultry or for the dog to be taken (on a leash, one must add) amongst poultry and given refresher courses in breaking to poultry frequently and possibly daily. It is worth noting that even if a dog merely disturbs chickens or ducks (and ducks are so easily disturbed) and puts them off-lay the owner of the dog may well be sued for damages. Turkeys are often hysterical at the sight of a skulking dog and hysterical turkeys have an incredible way of piling atop one another until the bottommost turkey is suffocated or crushed. It is essential that a lurcher is broken to livestock if the dog is to be used for hunting, for an unbroken dog is not only an unmitigated pest but a liability of the first order.

Getting a dog steady to bullocks and horses is an entirely different process for, whereas chickens, ducks, turkeys and sheep invariably take flight when a dog appears, ponies and bullocks are more likely to seek out the dog and in some cases attack it. At the time of writing I own a heavy hunter colt, a none too judicious mix of Clydesdale and Thoroughbred and this youngster is more than willing to take the fight to a dog. My own lurchers live in terror of the colt and hastily disappear when the horse starts to menace them. Dogs brought by visitors are in deadly danger for the colt follows up his warning with a ferocious display of hooves and teeth.

Bullocks are also a great danger to the lurcher, particularly if the lurcher is accompanied by a lamping group, for bullocks are incredibly curious animals and the appearance of a light attracts them and causes them to investigate the source of the beam. Dogs of all breeds are somewhat less than happy when ringed by a group of curious bullocks and are often panicked into bolting when a group of cattle approach them. One Midland estate that specialises in rearing Friesian bull calves also lets the estate to a small shooting syndicate that stocks the land with gamebirds. The land is not only heavily poached but each year a dozen or so lurchers are found wandering on the farmland, lurchers that have been separated from their owners when a group of cattle has disturbed the lamping party.

It is however lunacy to encourage lurchers to defend themselves against cattle and horses – though many lurchers will retaliate when they are harassed by farm livestock. It is far better policy for the lurcherman to call in his dogs as soon as cattle or horses appear and leash up lurchers before leaving the field where the stock is grazing. Further hunting will certainly not be productive in a field where cattle or horses have chased a frightened lurcher.

Obedience training should always precede entering a lurcher to quarry. Once a dog is entered and truly wed to quarry further obedience training becomes difficult.

8

General Principles of Entering to Quarry

No aspect of fieldsports invites such a variety of comments as the subject of entering a lurcher to quarry. Each and every lurcherman has his own method of entering a young lurcher or long dog and some of the methods advised are not only curious, bizarre and outlandish but illegal and certain to bring about a prosecution of the perpetrator and the defamation of fieldsports.

Rabbits are the principal quarry a lurcher is expected to hunt and it seems logical that a young lurcher should therefore be entered to this quarry. However, even this subject of first entering a lurcher to rabbit is questioned by some. E. G. Walsh, in his *Lurchers and Long-dogs* suggests that should a lurcher or long dog be required first and foremost as a single-handed hare courser (and more on this subject later) then the handler would be wise to eschew the use of rabbits to enter his hound. Rabbits are sprinters, running a brief 25 yard dash before finding refuge in a convenient burrow. Walsh argues, quite logically, that a hound that has pace and stride enough to outrun and catch a brown hare – one of the most taxing species in the world for a sighthound to course and catch – is frustrated by the flight of a rabbit – a species more suitable for a dog with a short sharp burst of speed to chase and catch. To a certain extent I must agree with Walsh for there is something very disconcerting about the sight of a long dog with a bewildered look on its face staring down a hole into which a rabbit has disappeared. Yet rabbits are readily available and are often used to prepare long dogs and sighthounds for the more exacting task of coursing hares. Rabbit hunting certainly sharpens a running dog and enables it to learn the task of picking up moving quarry. If the rabbits can be bolted from cover some distance from the main burrow or the playholes blocked, then rabbits are ideal quarry for starting a dog that is intended to be used as a single handed hare courser. Aficionados of match running, and this term too will be explained later – such as Don Southerd and the colourful Hughie Weaver – allow their dogs to hunt and catch rabbits before they are allowed to course hares. Southerd believes that any practice at catching quarry is preferable to no practice at all and allows his long dogs to course any rabbits they hunt up.

Many lurcher trainers swear by slipping a lurcher at a ferreted rabbit as a means of entering a lurcher; once again, this method has much to commend it. Normally the young lurcher is restrained with a slip while the burrow is ferreted and the lurcher is slipped at any rabbit that bolts before the ferret. This method affords the lurcher a chance to catch the bolting rabbit – but it is never easy to catch a rabbit that is bolting before a ferret. The majority of rabbits know exactly where they are heading when they bolt and manage to run to another warren or playhole to escape the lurcher. Rabbits are in fact seldom the easy meat many lurcher enthusiasts claim them to be. If rabbits were easy to catch the species would not be as numerous as it is in Britain, for the rabbit is the Ishmael amongst British mammals.

A far more common method of starting a lurcher puppy is by lamping the rabbit and allowing the puppy to chase the rabbit as it runs illuminated by the beam of light. Rabbits feed quite a distance from the burrow when darkness falls and hence the puppy is afforded a more lengthy run in order to attempt to catch the rabbit. Some lurcher puppies take almost instinctively to lamping while others take longer to associate the beam with the presence of rabbits. If, however, the puppy is allowed to see another dog run down the beam and catch a rabbit the whelp soon learns to watch the beam of light as it tracks around the field. Southerd also starts and sharpens his long dogs prior to a match running them on lamped rabbits, though the complex saluki/greyhound strain of long dog kept by him is bred to compete in single-handed hare coursing matches. Frankly as the majority of lurchers kept today are run at lamped quarry (the ethics of running certain quarry with the use of artificial light will be discussed later), starting a lurcher at lamped quarry is a fairly logical method of entering.

Allowing a lurcher to enter at its own pace – not aided by artificial lights or ferrets – is fairly logical if a somewhat lengthy method of entering, and is certainly beneficial to both dog and owner. Both have time to learn bushcraft – a quality seldom required by the lamper and his dog – and the puppy is usually allowed to catch at its own pace and when it is both physically and mentally ready for entering. Poachers and warreners alike were prone to adopt this method of entering and few pre-war lurcher keepers ever jack-knifed their dogs into premature entry. What is more important is the fact that this type of entering was often a lengthy process and allowed the handler to be able to understand the strengths and weaknesses of his particular dog and develop a bond with the lurcher. The modern lurcher is often badly treated, swopped, traded, bought and sold by a dozen owners each perhaps less understanding than the last. This dog-swapping is, however, a relatively modern malaise for pre-war lurchers were seldom subjected to such treatment.

It is however necessary to mention yet one more method of entering a lurcher to quarry before leaving the subject of starting the lurcher puppy. The practice of placing a live rabbit in front of a lurcher puppy and allowing the puppy to chase, catch and kill the rabbit would seem repugnant to any sane and sensible person. Yet the action, while it is clearly deplorable, is not illegal and occupies one of those shadowy grey areas of British law. If the rabbit is not injured, mutilated or in an exhausted state, nor restricted by ropes, chains or other devices to prevent its escape then no offence is being committed, but the terms 'captive or in a state of confinement' actually invites anyone who is witnessing the act of turning a live wild rabbit loose before a dog to bring a private prosecution against the perpetrator of the atrocity, and atrocity certainly describes the action accurately.

Atrocity is indeed the correct word for the practice which would certainly not be condoned by any sporting body. Firstly, a rabbit released in unfamiliar country will either panic and run wildly or, and this is more likely, simply squat and hope to remain unnoticed (this action is commonly practised by wild rabbits and at the start of the lamping season roughly thirty per cent of all rabbits adopt this stance rather than fleeing for home when they are illuminated by a beam of light). In point of fact this is an effective method of evading attack from a young dog, and possibly from a young fox, for inexperienced canids often appear confused when they encounter rabbits that refuse to move. Cub foxes will often nose a rabbit to cause it to run before seizing and killing the creature. Thus the act of turning a wild rabbit loose before a lurcher can not

A warrener with his lurcher in the 1920s.

David Hancock, the outstanding breeder of collie lurchers, with a litter of well-socialized, three-quarter bred collie/greyhound hybrids.

Below: A lurcher made to hold its dummy – an important accessory in retrieving training.

Jim Bell's collie/grey-hound hybrid jumping a fence.

Below: three dogs held at the sit position.

Canaan, the author's saluki/ greyhound bitch, a top winner as a courser, a superb jumper.

High jumping at Chatsworth in 1992. A strong, healthy lurcher seldom finds even a 12 ft leap any trouble.

Above: The author's Fathom – a great winner of early lurcher tests – who developed an amazing technique of catching feeding rabbits. *Below*: Collie crosses mark a warren. The various marking techniques can be highly informative to the handler.

Above: A lurcher steady to ferret. Ferreters' dogs take at least two years of hard work to train.

Breaking a lurcher puppy to ferret. It is important that lurcher puppies perceive ferrets as allies.

Picking up a hare is not always easy.

Below: A fox taken by lurcher/terrier combination. Brawls between lurchers and terriers are all too common in this situation.

Above: David Hancock's stud dog Richard Jones – to date the most potent force in lurcher breeding history. *Below*: Another of David Hancock's stud dogs, a collie famous for lurcher breeding.

only be barbaric and, despite the law, a damnably cruel action but slightly counter-productive to the training of the lurcher puppy.

I must confess I have often taken my lurcher puppies to places where myxomatosis is known to have broken out in the hopes that the puppy will be able to catch a rabbit that is incapacitated by the disease – unsporting perhaps, but a puppy needs a lot of help to catch its first rabbit. However, in some ways even starting a lurcher at a diseased rabbit is not an infallible method of entering a puppy. In the early stages of the disease an infected rabbit will run wildly when it is pursued by a dog, often running off country, away from rather than towards a burrow. Dogs will readily and eagerly pursue such animals, but as the disease progresses infected rabbits not only lose body weight and become almost skeletal in appearance but refuse to run when approached by a dog. Infected rabbits will often sit as tightly as squatters illuminated by a lamping kit and in many ways this mannerism is biologically helpful to the individual rabbit and thus to the species. Infected rabbits that recover from the disease often pass through the stage when they are unwilling to run and remain in this state for five or six days before displaying crust covered sores along the hind legs, anus, eyes and genitals. Some of these infected squatters become repulsive to touch and even some mustelids are reluctant to attack and eat them. Yet many of these rabbits survive the ravages of the disease and regain health and vigour as the winter continues.

Whatever the method of entering a lurcher to quarry, the handler must avoid committing any act of cruelty that will bring lurcherwork and fieldsports into disrepute and it must always be remembered that once a lurcher is entered to quarry further obedience training of the whelp in the field becomes difficult if not impossible.

There is absolutely nothing to be gained by entering the whelp prematurely and quite a lot to lose. The boasts of hunters who claim to have entered the whelp at the age of four months should be discounted and it is interesting to note that such lurchers are often sold by the time they are a year old. Training must precede entering or the lurcher becomes a liability rather than a pleasure to own. Comments passed by proud lurchermen as their untrained brute runs over the horizon and refuses to return, such as 'He'll come back when he's ready' tells the tyro lurcherman a lot about the training the wilful lurcher has been given. It is small wonder why the lurcher fraternity is viewed with suspicion by the landowners and farmers over whose land these untrained half-mad lurchers will run. It is the duty of every lurcher owner to have dogs that are obedient and biddable long before the they are ever given the chance to chase a rabbit.

9

Single-handed Hare Coursing

It is expedient to describe the training and entering of the single-handed hare coursing lurcher and long dog before describing the more complex skills a lurcher or long dog may be taught.

Basically, single-handed hare coursing involves slipping a single dog at a hare, and match running – a very hot potato at the time of writing – involves allowing the hare law (a fair start) of 80–100 yards before slipping the dog at the hare and sometimes wagering on the outcome of the course. Match running is often criticised by conventional coursers but match running, if conducted under fair and rigid rules, is perhaps one of the fairest and most testing fieldsports imaginable.

Despite the ridiculous claims made by lurchermen a dog is sorely tested by the athletic ability of a strong, fully grown brown hare and if the hare is afforded fair law few dogs will be able to catch it. Indeed few dogs will come to terms with the creature. The brown hare is not only a remarkable athlete, but an acrobat of the first order, able to dodge and duck with the alacrity of a flyweight and evade the strike of all but the most dextrous and experienced long dog or sighthound.

It is popular practice for the advocates of conventional coursing to describe match running as unsporting – but this is a ludicrous suggestion. Conventional coursing is conducted by running a pair of dogs at a hare, match running involves slipping only one dog at the quarry. It is argued that conventional coursing is conducted not to kill the hare but to test the mettle of the dogs pursuing the hare. Match running too is conducted to test the mettle of the dog, but the match running dog is required to catch rather than simply course the hare. Furthermore, it is doubtful if the hare understands or cares about the motives of the owners of the dogs pursuing it and it should also be noted that coursing sighthounds are not run muzzled and also try their best to kill their hares. It has been argued that wagering on the death of a hare is immoral yet gambling has always been an integral part of coursing – as the spate of bookmakers at most coursing meets attest. The coursing fraternity would in fact be well advised to study the match runner and his chosen pursuit before criticising the activity.

The act of walking a field, long dog on slip, and releasing the dog once a hare has risen and attained fair law is simplicity itself and requires no advice on how to perform the act, though few match runners have any idea of how far 100 yards really is. However getting a dog fit enough to not only come to terms with but to turn the hare before finally catching it is a complex skill without knowledge of which no coursing enthusiast should ever slip a dog at a hare.

Hares are some of the most amazing creatures the Almighty has ever designed. Although few hares grow larger than eight pounds in weight they are tremendous athletes that are capable of out-running most dogs. Take-off speed, final velocity and an incredible stamina all gel to produce the world's finest mammalian athlete and once the winter has winnowed the weak, the stupid, the unhealthy and the elderly from the hare population, the survivors – the January or Christmas hare that has lost much of its body fat and is lean, alert and fit – are able to out-pace, out-dodge and elude even the fastest of dogs. If a dog has speed enough to come to terms with a hare, it seldom has stamina to continue the course and capture the hare. If it has speed and stamina the dog seldom has brain enough to unravel the curious circuitous route the hare runs when under pressure from a dog and then at exactly the right moment to reach and snap up its quarry. An unusual amalgam must be present in the make up of a top-grade match dog for it must have speed, stamina and that indefinable something called coursing sense. Above all the dog must be subjected to a superb conditioning programme to make it ready to run and capture a fair law January hare.

The majority of match dogs are saluki/greyhound composites, animals which in theory should have the speed and early pace of a greyhound coupled with the stamina for which the saluki is famed. Some other mixes are added to the alloy, collie, Bedlington and even whippet blood but as match dogs become more and more proficient at their skills the rough or broken coat of the mongrelised long dog becomes less common and it appears that the majority of top flight match running long dogs boast a pedigree of three-quarter greyhound and a quarter saluki and at this point it is wise to state that in a properly conducted match a dog that will capture one in three January hares that have been afforded fair law will usually win a match. Tales of dogs consistently able to run and catch six consecutive fair law hares should be treated with some caution – and this is a magnificent understatement.

Sagar, a coursing aficionado with an enviable field record, was once approached by a man, mongrel long dog on leash, who asked how many hares Sagar expected his saluki to run in a day. At that time Sagar fielded a white smooth-coated bitch he called Annie who, despite her rather ordinary name, was bred in the purple out of the very best imported stock and had been runner-up in the Grieve Cup after a very impressive year in the coursing field. After a few moments Sagar replied that if his bitch was in peak condition and the courses were not too strenuous he would expect Annie to run as many as six hares in a day's coursing. The long dog enthusiast burst into a bout of derisive laughter and stated that he expected his long dog to run as many as sixteen or seventeen hares during a day's hare coursing. The fact is that many long dogs enthusiasts are totally out of touch with reality and are the most extraordinary liars. What is more terrifying is the fact that they pass on these lies to newcomers to the lurcher scene who believe the rubbish spoken by these outrageous liars and then become disenchanted by the perfomances of their own long dogs when the said animals are fielded against strong hares which have been afforded fair law. If a dog is fielded in a strong powerful condition, the hares are strong and are given 100 yards start, and it is an exceptional dog that can catch two out of three hares. Most best-of-three matches run to rules against seasoned winter hares are won by dogs that have caught one out of three hares. Readers who hear of dogs that seldom miss a hare, dogs that regularly catch six out of six hares they run should close their ears to such nonsense and disregard the teller of such tales.

It is worth noting just how many hares are killed at the Waterloo Cup where sixty-four of the finest greyhounds in the world, dogs that are superbly bred animals, trained to perfection, are run as couples against driven hares. If two of the very fastest greyhounds are seldom able to catch the hare they are attempting to course it is unlikely that a single-handed coursing long dog will knock down five out of six hares during a morning's coursing. One of the silliest things any long dog enthusiast can do is to underestimate the athletic prowess of a brown hare. Most dogs are over-matched by this seven pound athletic miracle.

However to condition a long dog to a state where it will put up a creditable performance against a brown hare is a great art. A long dog is seldom strong enough or wise enough to be truly conversant with the technique of hare catching before its second season and the reader would do well to discount tales of wonder dogs regularly catching strong hares in their first season. Indeed, if offered a young dog that has supposedly caught a great many hares before its first birthday, the would-be buyer should tread carefully for young dogs that are run at strong hares are usually so over-matched that they are physically and mentally damaged by the experience. Walsh in his 'Lurchers and Long dogs' states he believes a long dog, lurcher or sighthound should never be run at a hare before the dog is eighteen months of age and well grown – and Walsh is probably correct as the number of exhausted, tired, bewildered and prematurely aged long dogs doing the rounds of the dog dealers all too readily attests.

When the sapling is eighteen months of age it should be conditioned prior to its entry to the coursing field. Whether or not the long dog should have had experience at catching rabbits by day or by dint of a lamp has been discussed previously, but no dog that has not been specially conditioned should be slipped at a strong hare that is afforded 100 yards law. Conditioning should start six weeks before the coursing season begins and dogs that have been allowed to lie idle for the summer should start their training programme by brisk walking and allowing the dog to canter and play with another athletic dog. It has been argued that many dogs are injured as a result of collisions between two long dogs at play but there is no denying that two dogs will exercise more efficiently than a single dog allowed to romp and play with its owner.

A week or so of light training should precede the serious training programme and there are many methods of getting a coursing long dog ready for its tasks in the coursing field. Lamping rabbits is an excellent way of building up speed and stamina in a long dog, but no long dog should be allowed to run the beam in country where it might incur hurt or damage and the British countryside bristles with death-traps that can bring down the unwary dog. A brush against a barbed wire tine can cause a rip that can eviscerate an animal, a ridge of frozen earth or a surface stone will knock-up toes and render a long dog hors de combat for weeks. Over-exertion during the early days of the lamping season should also be avoided and a coursing dog should never be run until it starts to wilt.

Southerd of Burton-on-Trent regularly exercises his long dogs by allowing them to canter behind his Landrover at a brisk fifteen miles per hour until they are scarcely breathing hard after a fifteen minute exercise period, and only when his long dogs have arrived at this state of fitness does Don consider they are ready to field at strong hares. Southerd is a past-master at conditioning a long dog and has learned by long and testing experience that prowess of the strong winter hares against which he fields his dogs.

Exercise alone however is not enough to condition the match running dog and the reader may now realise that the long dog rather than traditionally bred lurchers is used for match running, for the modern match dog is a star's flight technique-wise from his pre-war counterpart. Match runners and conventional coursers alike have acquired much knowledge from the studies of Belgian pigeon racers. These fanciers noticed that when pigeons were raced over short distances, 30–100 miles, the birds raced best on a low protein/high carbohydrate mixture (wheat, maize, millet but small quantities of nitrogen rich pulses). As the length of the races increased, 100–600 miles, it was noticed that birds did better when the protein level of their diet was increased and the carbohydrate content of the diet reduced. It is interesting to note that Belgian pigeon racers had acquired the knowledge of diet long before trainers of human athletes or greyhound racers.

It was the custom of pre-war match runners to reduce their animals to a near skeletal condition and then flesh-out the animal prior to a match. This was, in fact, a technique used by dog fighters who were accustomed to matching dogs at a certain weight and as the Black Country conditioning programme for pit-fighting dogs was similar to that adopted by whippet racers, match runners too fed a poor diet to reduce the weight and tone of the animal and then fed a high protein diet to produce a dog of the required weight to fight or run. Most pre-war single-handed hare coursing dogs would have stood little chance of winning against even a mediocre long dog of today however.

Modern practice tends to favour taking up a dog from its summer rest period – a time when it has lived on a high carbohydrate and medium protein diet – and increasing the protein content of the diet as the dog's training programme progresses. A long dog at rest thrives quite well on a 20 per cent protein diet. but as the dog begins its training programme the proteinous content of its diet should be increased gradually until the animal is fed a diet which contains 27–32 per cent protein when the hare coursing season is at its peak and the dog is coursing some two days a week. Tissue is damaged when the dog is engaged in the furious pursuit of a hare and this tissue needs replacing by high class protein if the dog is to remain fit and well throughout the coursing season.

However top-grade best beef is not really essential feed for the coursing dog – indeed the meat is somewhat lacking in mineral content to be ideal. Cheap cuts of beef, mutton or horse meat are equally nutritious and a great deal less expensive. Rabbit and hare meat is in fact equally as nutritious and easily digested when cooked or fed raw. Match runners often indulge in the extravagant practice of stripping every morsel of fat from the meat they feed their match dogs but this is not only pointless but slightly counter-productive. Running dogs need a certain amount of fat in their diet to help the digestion of the meat. Excessively fatty meat is not desirable but the practice of stripping every fragment of fat from the meat to be fed is ludicrous.

It is customary never to feed a match running dog immediately prior to a coursing meet – indeed a full stomach is never conducive to the athletic performance of any species of animal. However the notion that a match dog needs to be starved for as long as forty-eight hours prior to running is erroneous. A twelve hour fast before a course allows a dog to be sharp set, empty gutted but still strong and fit enough to run well when slipped at a hare. Many match runners do not feed twenty-four hours before a coursing meet but give the dog an egg beaten up in milk some twelve hours before the dog is required to perform. Long fasts before a coursing meet will usually result in a dog wilting badly when it comes on a strong hare. Few match runners, or rather few successful match runners, resort to these extraordinary fasts these days but pre-war match runners often fasted a dog for far too long prior to a match. However, few pre-war match runners would justify a place on the field against today's match running greats.

Many, many dogs are injured while coursing – and damaged unnecessarily one should add. Before and after every course the handler should examine and note the condition of his dog. A dog that is still panting from the exertion of its last run should never be slipped at a hare. Neither should a dog that is swaying as a result of exhaustion nor a long dog that has a glazed expression on its face. Such animals have obviously been run too hard and need to be rested – not for an hour or so but for the rest of the week. Sadly many dogs that are sorely exhausted will still run at a hare but if fielded in the condition just described many dogs are permanently ruined. It is a sad indictment that many long dog and lurcher buffs boast of owning dogs that have died while coursing. The majority of these dogs had displayed obvious warning signs long before their demise, but these warning signs had not been heeded by the handler. If a dog is a shade under-par, a shade off-colour, it is madness to match this dog against the world's greatest mammalian athlete. Serious match runners, top-grade conditioners and trainers, will concede defeat and withdraw an over-run or unwell dog from competition, for to compete with such an animal is not only a guarantee of defeat but is fairly certain to permanently injure the dog. Some long dog experts have an inbuilt ability to know all is not well long before the dog manifests obvious symptoms of distress. In 1980 I watched Southerd field his now famous bitch, Lady, a saluki/greyhound composite with a minute quantity of spaniel blood. The bitch ran a strong hare at Tamworth, Staffordshire, and lost the hare after a lengthy and gruelling course. She returned to Don scarcely winded but Southerd refused to run her again despite the chiding of his companion. Southerd knew the strengths and weaknesses of his animal and had decided the bitch was not ready for another run. Lady became a famous bitch and seldom let Don down during her long and active life. Her contests against Tom Brown's fabulous Anna now belong in match dog history. It is interesting to compare Southerd's attitude with that of the braggart who approached Paul Sagar with a tale of sixteen runs at hare in an afternoon.

Few dogs are capable of daily runs at hare without inflicting serious damage on themselves. Two days' coursing a week or three days a fortnight is usually enough to tax the physical resources of the best conditioned long dog. If a dog is run too regularly the animal invariably loses its edge and tries less hard during a course or runs half-heartedly. Saluki hybrids which are renowned for their stamina are also the first to suffer when run too regularly at strong hares. The best athletes are often animals which come into top form perhaps once or twice a week and then give their all for three or four muscle-aching courses at hares, but a top class dog run too often will easily degenerate into an average dog that never really gives its best. The hare is such a wonderful athlete that a dog is easily over-taxed, strained and mentally demoralised if run too regularly at hares. Few top-grade match runners will field their best dog more than twice a week even when the hares are plentiful and the conditions over which the dogs are to run are ideal. At one time Jeff Smith who owned the famous Fly, mother and grandmother of some of today's top match runners, set aside two days of his working week to course, but seldom ventured out of doors with his top dogs except to walk or exercise them. Smith had the knack of conditioning his dogs to a nicety and never running a dog unfit or a shade below-par.

To take a successful dog that has run three hard testing runs at hare, to place that dog in a kennel and forget about the animal until the next time it is required for coursing is an extremely short-sighted practice. Once the dog has recovered from its exertions it needs an easily digested high-grade proteinous feed to repair bruised and damaged muscles that have been taxed, strained or injured after its course at the hares it has been required to chase – and incidentally a long dog may lose as much as six pounds in weight after a hard and taxing day's coursing. It is in fact possible to see how ribby a hitherto well-fleshed dog appears after three testing runs at hares. The dog needs a high protein, easily digested meal to replace these torn muscle cells and this meal should consist of cooked rabbit, chicken, or if the dog enjoys the food, carefully boned fish. Some professional coursers simply feed a 32 per cent proteinous dog meal to an animal that has had a hard and testing day's coursing.

I must confess I have little experience as to how effective electrolyte solutions are in affecting a running dog's recovery from a hard, testing day's coursing. Electrolyte sachets consist of various salts similar in content to the solution in which muscles are bathed and also a sachet of glucose. These electrolytes are very efficient at preventing dehydration in an animal that has suffered from alimentary disorders and is scouring badly, but electrolyte solutions are relatively new to the world of match running. Coursing and racing greyhounds are often given solutions of these mineral salts/glucose sachets after hard and testing courses and races. They are certainly well received by the exhausted dog and I have seen spent dogs take on a new lease of life after ingesting a solution made from these electrolyte sachets. Furthermore I have yet to hear an unfavourable report concerning giving these solutions to an exhausted dog.

The elaborate conditioning, medication and feeding of a top class long dog should alert the reader to the dangers of taking good class coursing long dogs from kennels after they have been fed or are not in top condition. To run such a dog unprepared simply because a friend arrives and suggests a day's coursing is to court disaster. More dogs are ruined by impromptu coursing capers than the reader might imagine. Only when a dog is fit and ready and in top running form should a long dog be fielded against strong winter hares.

A long dog run in condition, suitably fasted though not starved on the day of the course, should on returning from the meet be almost ravenously hungry and will usually have to be restrained from wolfing down totally unsuitable food. A dog that takes only a moderate interest in food after a day's coursing, or worse still, a long dog that disdains food, should be suspect, for something is clearly amiss. Long dogs fresh from the coursing field should display a typical gluttony and then lapse into an almost comatose-like sleep. A long dog that shows an interest only in sleeping when it returns from the field should be regarded as unwell. Damage to the heart, lungs and diaphragm are all too frequent amongst match dogs that have had one run too many and the symptoms of damage to these organs are usually that the dog displays unusual lassitude and reluctance to feed. The majority of successful match runners are, at the risk of appearing indelicate, urine watchers – men who observe the colour, scent and nature of the urine passed by a dog that has run a series of hard and testing courses. Quite pungent, strong scented urine is normal when a hard worked long dog has experienced a more than tough course, for tissues undergo great chemical changes when a dog is subjected to very strenuous exercise and the breakdown products of damaged muscle tissue are often quite unpleasant to the smell. However few healthy dogs will pass these breakdown products two or three days after a coursing event and should the animal still be passing foetid urine, or displaying an unusual roached back posture while it urinates, all is far from well and the dog is clearly in need of veterinary attention. It is quite impossible for the dabbler, the dog swapper, the instant expert lurcherman to realise just how injurious a succession of runs after strong hares can be to the constitution of a dog – and long dogs are usually game enough to run even when they are experiencing desperate pain and distress. Many long dogs die prematurely because of this do-or-die disposition, but many of these dogs could have been saved by timely veterinary intervention.

The long dog often leads an incredibly hard life – particularly if the animals are run regularly in country that is well stocked with strong hares, and if subjected to regular long and strenuous courses many long dogs age rapidly. Injuries commonly bring a premature end to otherwise promising coursing careers, toes are often knocked up, wrists are strained by the terrific exertion employed to run strong hares and peculiarities known as dropped muscles are sustained by many long dogs – particularly greyhound-saturated types of long dogs, so it appears. For some reason, possibly because of the laid-back running style of many Middle Eastern types of sighthound, saluki composites, or rather, long dogs with more than just a trace of saluki in their ancestry, are not only more durable but also have a slightly longer field life that do long dogs of Celtic greyhound origin – whippet/greyhound, deerhound/greyhound composites. Deerhound/greyhound hybrids, despite their incredible beauty, have a reputation for having quite a short field life. They seldom give of their best before their fourth season and are well and truly spent before their seventh year. To compensate for their short coursing life these hybrids are, however, the most intelligent and elegant of long dogs and are easier to live with than saluki long dogs many of whom appear resistant to obedience training. Whippet/greyhound hybrids are now seldom seen on the match field – though at one time they were the most popular hybrid for such competitions – also have reputations for affording the match runner a longer coursing life, but the hybrid, alas, has a reputation for being very injury prone. It is worth concluding this chapter with a somewhat unpleasant though all too apt quote from that doyenne of hunting, the Abbess Juliana Berner, who in 1486 wrote her rather merciless *Boke of St. Albans* and says of the greyhound:

> But when he has come to his seventh year
> Get him to a tanner.

It might be worth adding that a prematurely entered long dog run often unfit will be ready for the tanner long before its seventh season!

10

Working the Lurcher by Day

The word poacher is often wrongly used and many so-called country poachers are simply mouchers, Autolycus figures, snappers-up
of unconsidered trifles. The true poachers, the poaching gangs of
Victoriana, seldom used lurchers. They arrived on estates, denuded
the said estates of all saleable game, and then returned to the towns
from whence they came to sell their swag to unscrupulous game
dealers. Poachers filch game in quantity, wiping out huge stocks
of hares, rabbits, pheasants and partridge. The moucher was an
entirely different sub-species. He seldom lived outside the district
he worked and picked up the game from nearby estates – he was
regarded as a nuisance rather than a menace, a curiosity rather than
a dangerous criminal. If encouraged he, no doubt, sold some of his
catch but he was always simply the man to 'see about a hare' rather
than the villain who caught game in vast quantities to sell to dealers.
It was the moucher rather than the poacher who bred and used the
lurcher, and working at night without the use of artificial lights or
making daytime forays into forbidden estates, the moucher and his
lurcher would have secured small hauls for their efforts.

The fact is, that a dog allowed to hunt up an estate during
daylight hours will seldom catch a large head of game. Pheasants
and partridge are always alert when they forage for feed, rabbits
seldom feed far from their homes during the daylight hours and
hares, well, hares are the most difficult of creatures to catch when
the lurcher enthusiast and his dog are not aided by artificial lights
or nets. Thus the truly competent lurcher enthusiast who works
by day allowing his lurchers to hunt up game by scent/sight will

never catch a fraction of the game a lamper with few skills and a badly trained lurcher will secure by night. However, with the right training and with that indefinable quality known as bushcraft the daytime lurcherman can greatly increase his haul.

Dawn and dusk are favoured times for lurchermen to venture abroad, for in the half-light rabbits will still be feeding far from their warrens, hares will be intent on seeking the night's food, or at dawn be bloated with the feed they have ingested the night previous, partridge are still settled into watchful coveys and pheasants are either preparing to fly to their perches or are ravenously feeding after a night's fast in the trees. Thus at dawn and dusk the lurcherman should venture abroad with his dog.

It is a curious fact that since the war-time years lurchers seem to be shy of catching and carrying feathered quarry. Many theories are offered why this is so – and one of the most logical of these theories suggests that the old type of lurcher, the traditional companion of the moucher, has long since gone the way of the dodo. Many lurcher strains have become so infused with sighthound blood that they might be classed as long dogs rather than true lurchers, and while these dogs might snap up the occasional pheasant, the winged bird or the unwary Phasian as it explodes from the grass, or catch the wounded partridge that fails to whir into flight, many modern lurchers show an indifference to hunting up feathered game.

There are several methods of starting lurchers to feathered game, many of which smack of witchcraft and should be disregarded. One of the most logical methods of entering a dog to feather was practiced by Moses Smith and was said to be a common method of entering to feather amongst the Kentish Romany. A dead pheasant was drawn on a 'cat and mouse' line in front of the puppy and the whelp encouraged to mouth and pick up the feathered carcase. Various birds could be used to encourage the dog to chase feather but jackdaws and pigeon were not favoured by those who advocated this method of entering. Puppies of all breeds – even some spaniels – often show a marked reluctance to mouth pigeon carcases. There are some instances of spaniel puppies that have developed such a distaste for picking up pigeons that they have refused to carry any form of feathered game.

When the whelp was frantic to seize the pheasant carcase a pheasant was thrown and the whelp encouraged to fetch the corpse. Later when the puppy was considered obedience trained enough to come to hand quickly it was taken to the edge of rides pheasants were known to frequent and encouraged to hunt up the gamey scent. In passing I should mention that at the time of writing I am training a young lurcher puppy I call Phaedra, a bitch that is more keen to hunt feather than fur, however she runs larks with the same enthusiasm as she hunts conventional game. Young dogs, setters, pointers and dual purpose retriever/pointer types will often point larks during their puppyhood, but eventually learn to differentiate between the scent of lark and more acceptable game.

Dogs are quite often mature before they succeed in becoming proficient at catching partridge, particularly the grey partridge. Partridge explode from grass or cover with a loud whirring sound – a biologically successful flight style the noise of which deters many predators. Dogs are often startled by the sound of the whirring flight of partridge and will often refuse to catch partridge – some indeed are chary of approaching a covey that springs into flight. Others are excited by the sound and strike wilily or carefully and succeed in bringing down at least one of the covey that is springing into flight. Phaedra, one of my young lurcher puppies, displays a mass of undesirable qualities but she is incredibly efficient at snapping at and grounding birds when a covey of partridge whirs into flight.

First forays against daytime rabbits are often not only futile but destructive to the morale of the lurcherman and his ward. I make a point to walk a puppy on the headland between the warrens and the place where rabbits are known to feed so that the whelp has an opportunity to intercept the rabbit as it flees for home. Here however is the rub. A rabbit racing towards the dog provides a far more difficult animal to catch than a rabbit that is racing away from the dog. A dog will in fact often make many morning and evening jaunts before it succeeds in catching a rabbit, but lurchers learn so much from their mistakes. Within months of this training the dog will no longer run rabbits wildly, driving all to ground before it succeds in catching a single rabbit, but stalk a potential catch and pursue its worthy victim remorselessly, forsaking all others. No short-cut entering methods succeed and nothing can replace experience. If a dog is subjected to this lengthy entering technique no matter how many mistakes it makes, no matter how many rabbits it misses, it nevertheless learns that quality known as bushcraft. I own one of the greatest exponents of bushcraft I have ever seen, a doddery, ancient animal called Fathom who despite her great age is still with me. Fathom missed many rabbits but learned an amazing technique of catching feeding coneys. She approached them on 'tippy-toe' using each bush to advantage, walking up and stalking the rabbit she had selected ignoring others, even rabbits she'd observed feeding nearer to her. She would inch forward remaining motionless when the rabbit gazed in her direction and making one short, sharp dash at her chosen quarry. Her success rate was exceptional but she took many years to learn and master this technique – and I hasten to add missed many, many rabbits during the learning process. Eventually she became so dextrous at exploiting this technique that photographers travelled many miles to film Fathom stalking rabbits. She was, however, over fourteen months old before she made her first catch – and took a great deal longer to learn the stalking technique that made her famous. It is interesting to note that her great great great great granddaughter is developing the same technique as did her ancestor, and is learning or acquiring this skill at the same painstakingly slow pace.

More interesting still is the way a lurcher learns to deal with a rabbit that has crouched in a patch of bramble and whose scent has alerted the lurcher to the presence of the rabbit. Young, inexperienced lurchers will invariably crash through cover and once tangled in the stolons of brambles appear dismayed at the sight of the rabbit high-tailing it to safety. As the lurcher becomes more experienced or develops a degree of bushcraft it begins to adopt an entirely different technique of dealing with a rabbit sitting in such a thorny fortress. The experienced lurcher will seldom crash through the thicket to attempt to secure its catch, but race around the thicket making feints into the tangle to frighten the rabbits to flight. Penguin, one of the ancestors of my strain of lurcher, became extraordinarily adept at flushing rabbits in this manner and caught a great many rabbits by this means. I notice that her great great great great great granddaughter, a three-legged bitch called Kyle, is beginning to perfect the same technique, at a somewhat greater rate one should add, for her awful injury has caused her to perfect the technique of catching bush rabbits quickly. These peculiar skills cannot be taught, neither can the trainer assist in the dog's acquisition of bushcraft. Experience, and experience tempered by persistent failure and a modicum of success, teaches bushcraft, but the acquisition of the skills are learned slowly and the dog experiences many cumbersome mistakes while certain skills are being acquired. There are no short-cuts to gain these skills, no instant training methods to put old heads on young shoulders and the only advice I can offer the trainer is to let the dog acquire the skills in silence and not to assist the animal with war-whoops to indicate the presence of the rabbit in the thicket.

Yells of encouragement are often difficult to restrain, but they are confusing to the dog and tend to encourage maladies such as false marking – and this imperfection will be explained shortly.

In areas thickly populated with rabbits young and medium-sized rabbits will often sit outside the burrows during the daylight hours in rank, dead grass or in rush beds either to play, or what is more than likely, to feed on dead grasses to add bulk to their diet. Woodlands adjoining lush clover pastures are often stripped of dead, unpalatable grasses by rabbits eager to balance the high nitrogenous feed with a low protein/high roughage diet. Whatever the reason why young rabbits adopt this practice, the rabbits offer sporting quarry to the lurcherman who is not assisted by a ferret. Lurchers hunting up these daytime sitters must also acquire a style of catching these sitting rabbits and this skill too must be acquired by trial and many, many errors. It is only a matter of time before even the least tractable lurcher realises that a headlong dash into clumps of dead grass that are likely to hold a rabbit will usually result in the rabbit racing for a burrow – the majority of which seem to appear out of thin air just in time to allow the rabbit to escape. It is always amazing how, when pursued by a lurcher, a rabbit manages to escape an apparently inevitable catch by disappearing down a rabbit hole a micro-second before the dogs snap up the fleeing coney. The fact is that as a rabbit nears the burrow it literally drops down a gear so as to be able to disappear into the burrow neatly and smoothly. The dog, unaware of the ploy, gains on the rabbit that now having gauged the entrance to the warren then quickens its pace and dives into the sanctuary of the burrow. I ask the reader to perform an experiment. Place an industrial glove on one hand and drive one's fist into the first rabbit burrow encounter. The obstructions in the burrow will usually cause considerable hurt and perhaps pain. By timing and gauging its entrance into the sanctuary hole the rabbit avoids such hurt – but gives the lurcherman watching the course the impression the lurcher is certain to catch the rabbit.

Many lurchers learn to cope with such erratic flight patterns and attempt rugby tackle type catches as the rabbit reduces its speed. This flying tackle is not without its dangers to the dog however, for most burrows are excavated on land that is elevated and often rocky.

Working a thickly populated rabbit infested area near wasteland on which tufts of grass or rush beds grow can be productive for the lurcherman – indeed I regularly work such a place where my lurchers can, and do, catch up to a score of rabbits during a day's hunting in such rush beds, but such productive areas are far from common throughout Britain.

Unlike the match running long dog, the pot filling lurcher must 'never give a sucker a break' where hare catching is concerned. Few conventional lurchers are in fact capable of putting up a creditable show against a strong winter hare that has been afforded fair law. At the time of writing I own the best lurcher bitch I have ever owned in my life, an animal that puts her ancestors to shame as hunting dogs. Her haul of hares is great, but she is totally incapable of catching a hare that has gained momentum. I am aware of this fact and, so I believe, is she, for should she observe a hare running in full flight a hundred or so yards away she will watch the spectacle with interest but decline to pursue the hare. In rough cover at the art of sneak attacks on sitting hares she is devastatingly efficient and has caught several hundred hares by the ploy she uses. In fact if asked for a cliché or an epigram to define the difference between a lurcher and a long dog I would say that a long dog will bring down a hare by dint of its athletic prowess, a lurcher brings down its hare by stealth and cunning.

Young lurchers, even highly intelligent lurchers, will attempt to catch each and every hare as the creature explodes from its form and experience alone will cause the dog to modify its technique to catch hares. As the youngster learns by mistakes it seldom adopts a headlong rush to catch an accelerating hare. Experienced dogs, dogs that have had many encounters with hares, will adopt amazing and fascinating ways of catching hares. Quimby of Lichfield once owned a bitch that had an incredible success rate at catching hares. When she observed a hare feeding at a great distance she adopted a cat-like stalking technique, walking towards the hare, stopping when the hare ceased feeding and raised it head, and resuming her stalk when the animal continued to feed. As she approached the hare she became more careful still, and viewed and assessed the escape route the hare would take before she made her final dash at the creature. Personally I found this stalking technique equally as exciting as full-blooded fair law courses – and frankly it was a dozen times as effective at securing hares. At fair law coursing she was often over-matched by saluki-bred long dogs, but she was mistress of her art.

At this point it might be expedient to mention the dichotomy that should exist between true lurchers and long dogs. At the time of writing there is still a tendency to mingle collie-bred lurchers with long dogs, particularly long dogs with a strong trace of saluki in their origin. This is a shortsighted breeding programme that is practised in an attempt to breed a good lurcher with a great deal of extra speed. In point of fact the product of such a union is usually something akin to a poor-grade long dog with none of the desired qualities of either parent. To adapt an old saying, 'what one loses on the swings one also loses on the roundabouts'. Most lurchers are capable of achieving the speed needed in a moucher's dog.

What is even more fascinating still is the technique developed by some dogs of running a hare off country, of pushing it off its conventional flight paths that invariably lead to deep cover or gaps in fences and hedges. A hare once pressured off its chosen paths panics and becomes easy meat – that is if a hare ever becomes easy meat for the lurcher to catch. Dogs that are capable of understanding this fact, or rather, dogs which for some reason show an innate understanding of how to bring down hares, are really quite rare.

In my youth a West Wales lurcherman called Rhys Rassendyl Rhys (he was born the year Hope Hawkins published *The Prisoner of Zenda*, so Tom Evans of Blaengarw assured me) owned a tremendous lurcher bitch that had little of the speed one associates with a great hare catching dog, but knew exactly how to head off hares from their flight paths. She had an uncanny gift of knowing exactly how a hare would run and how to intercept the hare before it ran through a gap in the hedge. I watched her run twice, once in Cardigan when she caught four or five hares which she had hunted up and made the technique look easy, and once in Gloucestershire where she was coursed at fair law hares. She failed dismally at this skill for while she had brain aplenty she lacked speed to come to terms with her hare. As a lurcher I have yet to see her equal, but she was not equipped to run hares that had fair law. What happened to this lurcher bloodline is still the subject of some speculation. Tale has it Vesey Fitzgerald was given one lurcher from this strain – and promptly published *It's My Delight* in which he stated that he believed the lurcher to be superior to the collie intelligence-wise. Another of this breeding went to one John Scopes, a relative of John Scopes one of the participants in the Dayton monkey trial of 1925. The line apparently became lost or bred-out after the outbreak of myxomatosis in 1953 – though Michael Lyne, the artist, once said that he believed some breeders still kept a related bloodline that produced ugly collie-like lurchers without class or symmetry. Lyne, however, was a perfectionist if the first order and admitted that he had never seen these lurchers hunt or course hares.

Infusions of sighthound blood – and most lurcher breeders add far too much sighthound blood to their strain of lurcher – do little to improve the hunting ability of the dogs. In fact many lurchers winning at today's lurcher shows are, despite their elegant, aesthetically appealing shape, little more biddable, intelligent or trainable than pure bred sighthounds or long dogs. Sadly when the first Lambourn lurcher show was staged in 1974 a rough standard of excellence seemed to have been drawn up by the lurcher judges of the time and dogs with far too much sighthound blood are now winning well at lurcher shows, animals bred with little thought to the baseline (non-sighthound portion of the lurcher) and are produced by simply mating more and more sighthounds into a strain of lurcher. The resultant product is virtually a long dog rather than a lurcher, though when Moses Smith, one of the judges of the 1981 Lambourn Show, passed such a comment his wisdom was met by the disapproval of the other judges. The trials now staged by the National Lurcher Racing Club may well reverse this sighthound-saturation process, for long dog-cum-lurcher hybrids are seldom trained well enough to compete at these trials. Neither have these sighthound-saturated lurchers the right attributes to make them suitably versatile hunters in the field.

11

Ferreting with Lurchers

It is possible for the punter, the 'buy-a-trained-dog' lurcher buff to visit any dog dealer who specialises in selling lurchers and purchase a lamping dog of sorts for fifty pounds or less. Off-the-peg lamp dogs are a dime a dozen, at the risk of mixing both metaphors and currency, though I have yet to see a satisfactorily trained lurcher come from any dealer's kennels.

However, I ask the reader to perform a simple and interesting experiment – visit the self-same dealer, or any lurcher dealer for that matter, and attempt to buy a competent, trained ferreter's dog and I will wager the reader will achieve no success in purchasing such a lurcher. He may well be offered a dog that is not actively hostile to ferrets, one that either ignores ferrets or does not kill a ferret on sight. He may be offered a dog that can be held on a slip while a ferret works its rabbit below ground, a dog that can be slipped as the rabbit bolts and even a dog that will catch a rabbit bolted by ferrets and return the said rabbit to hand. What the reader will not be offered is a dog that is steady, biddable, comes quickly to hand, marks inhabited burrows, freezes as the ferret works its rabbit below ground, ignores netted rabbits but runs escapers retrieving them neatly to hand. Such dogs are never, or hardly ever, offered for sale by the dog dealer, for dog dealers seldom train dogs but buy them trained, or slightly trained, from others who have tired of, or become disenchanted, with their dogs.

Ferreters' dogs take at least two years of hard work to train them. Two years of careful training to make them competent, so that they do not make the owner embarrassed when dog and handler take to the field. No one in his right mind will sell such an animal that has occupied his waking and sleeping thoughts for two years – at least not for the price the dealer is prepared to pay, and few dealers pay more than £20 or £30 for any animal they purchase. The majority of vendors who sell their lurchers to dealers are disappointed, embittered and upset with the poor performance or the poor training of the animal they are offering for sale and, hence, are prepared to part with the animal for a song – some will literally give their dogs to lurcher dealers to be rid of the wretched animals.

If the reader disbelieves what I say I ask him to take the experiment just one stage further. Ask the dealer to take the would-be buyer for a trial with the ferreter's dog he has for sale – avoid excuses that will pour like water from a fountain – and insist the dealer accompanies the buyer. The chances are the dog will not mark true (and if it does the dealer will have neither wit nor wisdom to be able to interpret the mark the dog is making). It is a racing certainty the dog will behave badly when a ferret is to ground and it is fairly certain that the dog will bite at the rabbits encased in the purse nets. Ferreters' dogs are oh so rarely offered for sale – they take so long to train and the process of training them is so complex that few hunters are prepared to part with the finished product at any price.

So, just what are the training modules the ferreter's dog must master during this long and rigorous training programme? Firstly, the dog must be biddable and return to hand instantly and without question. When a dog chases a rabbit that is bolted or perhaps slipped the net and misses the said rabbit, the dog that races to and fro regardless of the pleas of its owner is an absolute nuisance. Besides which the pleas of the handler will do little to convince the rabbit still in the burrow that it is safe to bolt. Hence, a disobedient dog, a rebellious dog that believes it knows best when running the scent of a rabbit is not desirable. A ferreter's dog should, on failing to catch its rabbit, run straight back to its handler, no matter how heavy the scent of the rabbit it has just missed.

The ferreter's dog must also remain steady either at the sit or lie position or frozen to immobility while the ferret works below ground, and must remain fixed until a rabbit bolts regardless of the distractions around it, be they sheep, cattle, horses or fragments of paper or debris blowing in the wind. Sit, lie, stay or freeze training (and I shall deal with the subject of freezing presently) is therefore essential. The majority of ferreter's dogs dart from hole to hole, scratching at warrens, sometimes barking, thereby alerting the rabbits to their presence regardless of the entreaties of their owners. In fact, in some forty years of ferreting I have seen only a handful of dogs that weren't an embarrassment to their ferreting owners. At one time so badly trained were the dogs of fellow ferreters that I came to the conclusion that these hunters regarded their dogs as somewhat unruly companions rather than helpmates.

A lurcher intended for ferreting work should have an excellent nose so as to be able to mark inhabited burrows. If a dog does not mark true then the ferreter must net up every set of holes in the hopes that one will be inhabited – and this is an extremely time-consuming and often fruitless activity. It is virtually impossible for a man to be able to tell if a burrow is inhabited by rabbits or simply a playhole into which rabbits will dart and play but seldom use on a permanent basis. It can be argued that a breeding or permanent burrow will seldom have a sprinkling of faecal matter in front of its entrances whereas playholes are usually liberally peppered with rabbit pellets. However, many, many times I have startled rabbits out feeding and observed some dart into playholes. I have, in fact, taken many rabbits from playholes when one of my lurchers has marked a rabbit that has used this set of burrows as a temporary refuge. A dog that will not mark true and accurately will not be a great deal of use as a ferreting dog. I cannot resist an anecdote to end this paragraph. One of the most competent marking dogs I have in my kennels is a saluki/greyhound that was trained and entered alongside a lurcher puppy of roughly the same age. My long dog became a highly proficient marker but because of its low attention span – a leaf stirring or blowing in the wind a hundred yards or so away totally absorbed her and she became bored with the activity taking place within the burrow – she became a somewhat less than suitable ferreter's dog. In fact, I have yet to see a long dog of any breeding that fulfilled my requirements as a ferreter's dog.

I have seen many non-retrieving lurchers taken along on ferreting forays and all have been unmitigated nuisances. When a rabbit finds an unguarded bolthole or slips a net and escapes, a ferreter's lurcher must pursue and attempt to catch the rabbit. If it succeeds in catching the rabbit (and this is seldom easy for where there are many rabbits there are many playholes into which a rabbit can run when pursued) the lurcher must retrieve its catch to hand instantly and without being called to hand. A lurcher that catches and stands over its kill causing the ferreter to leave the burrow that is still being worked by a ferret is counter-productive to the efficiency of a ferreting team. The dog that circles the handler, rabbit in mouth, is equally annoying though this malaise is usually due to the fact that another dog has also been worked alongside the lurcher – and hence the dog carrying the rabbit has become jealous of its catch. The catch must be brought quickly and also quietly to hand by the ferreter's lurcher without fuss or histrionics, that is, dropping the catch and allowing to run again – a common fault at the start of a ferreting season that is often self-correcting as the season progresses.

The technique of teaching a dog to sit, stay or lie has been described in an earlier chapter, but teaching the freeze technique of fixing a dog needs some explanation. While it is expedient to teach any dog to sit, lie or stay the freeze posture is certainly the most efficient way for the ferreter's dog to station itself above a warren when the ferret is working to rabbit. When a rabbit bolts and slips the net or finds that all too common unguarded hole and escapes, a dog placed at the down position is in a disadvantageous position if required to pursue the rabbit. Two distinct movements are needed for the dog that is stationed in the down position to be up and chasing the rabbit – and a split second usually gives the rabbit a decided edge over any pursuer. Likewise, a dog stationed at the sit position above or near the burrow where the ferret is working needs to rise before it can pursue a bolting rabbit and, as has been mentioned, a split second is all that is needed for the rabbit to escape capture.

Hence I teach the ferreter's lurcher to freeze above a burrow that is being ferreted. While the ferret is to ground I crouch with the puppy standing next to me and place my index finger against the elbow of the front legs and the chest to restrict the dog's movement. This pressure needs to be slight and the finger kept in position while the rabbit stays below ground. If I hear sounds that indicate the rabbit is likely to bolt – bumping, the sound of squealing or movement along the passageways of the burrows – I raise my other index finger and whisper 'Watch' in an excited fashion to the puppy. Excitement is so infectious that it takes only a short time for the puppy to associate the hushed whisper and the raised index finger with the appearance of a rabbit. As the training progresses I no longer restrict the movement of the puppy with the index finger pressed against its sternum, but should the whelp's interest begin to wane I still raise my hand and whisper 'Watch' to maintain the puppy's attention. It takes a very short time to teach the puppy to freeze when the ferret is working below ground, providing, that is, that the owner doesn't repeatedly fool the puppy by ferreting uninhabited warrens and uttering 'Watch' to the puppy while the ferret simply trundles through the empty burrow. Different dogs adopt different freeze postures and allowances must be made for this fact. Phaedra, my youngest lurcher bitch, adopts an upright stance, ears half erect, when she freezes. Canaan, my long dog, remains immobile, a glazed look on her face while Merab, my best lurcher bitch – the best I've ever owned in fact – freezes in a panther-like crouch, oblivious to everything except the movements within the warren. Merab is fascinating to watch but whether her particular style of freezing makes her more efficient or her greater experience gives that impression is open to question. Certainly the freeze position gives a dog an edge over the animal that is asked to sit, lie or stay.

Marking, or rather the teaching of, or the necessity to teach marking, is a controversial subject, but certainly one I feel qualified to discuss. My strain of lurcher has a reputation for being excellent at marking, partly due to their innate tendency to mark holes and partly due to the fact that they are taught to mark holes, or their tendency to mark holes is reinforced by certain techniques.

Konrad Lorenz in his book *King Solomon's Ring* introduced what at that time was considered to be a somewhat heretical notion that animals, and particularly domesticated animals, attempted to communicate with human beings. His opinions were subject to some disbelief as critics were wont to compare Lorenz's scientific works with the writings of Georg Schwidetsky who wrote the rather ludicrous book *Do You Speak Chimpanzee*, a best seller that produced a spate of zoo visitors who babbled gibberish at the cages of chimpanzees. Lorenz, however, was correct in the assumption that man with a notion to study the behaviour of beasts could understand what certain animals wished to convey to him. All that was needed, so to speak, was a Rosetta Stone, a key to the language in which certain animals were attempting to communicate with man.

I allow a dog every attempt to communicate with me, particularly where marking is concerned, but I help furnish my own Rosetta Stone. If a dog shows a natural inclination to mark an inhabited burrow, either by standing and pointing the hole or by gently scratching at the entrance of such a hole, I ferret the burrow the dog is marking. This action rewards the dog's efforts for if a rabbit bolts the dog sees some results for its marking the warren. The more the dog's efforts are rewarded by the sight of a rabbit bolting after the dog has marked a warren the more the marking technique is reinforced. My own bitch, Merab, will find a burrow that houses a rabbit in it and then deliberately seek me out to return with her so that I may ferret the burrow.

I believe that one of the best ways of learning how a dog is attempting to mark a warren is to watch a dog chase a rabbit into a burrow and observe how the dog behaves when the rabbit runs to ground. The sight of a rabbit run to ground observed by both the handler and the dog constitutes a Rosetta Stone, a means of interpreting the dog's marking gestures – and many dogs display a variety of gestures when marking a hole – I'll explain presently – since the handler knows the rabbit is to ground and so does the dog and the mannerisms displayed by the dog indicate that a rabbit is at home. Later these mannerisms will be refined a little and the owner must watch for these mannerisms as they undergo sublimation.

Regarding the various marking techniques which will tell the handler much about the inhabitants of the burrow, Merab, my own lurcher bitch, emits some sixteen different signals when a rabbit is to ground – and these signals have been subject to scientific testing and observed by several dozen hunters. A scratch at a hole means that a rabbit is in the earth and lying in a shallow gallery. A long meaningful stare into the earth means the rabbit is lying up in a rather deep gallery. An excited racing 'twixt the holes of a play burrow means the rabbit is considering bolting and moving about the galleries of the play burrow. A pause outside a burrow, a raised paw or a gesture which bespeaks some setter ancestry perhaps, means that the rabbit has just run to ground a few moments previous. Her tail, flagged, as with all her family, held out like a setter indicates a rabbit is in a very shallow earth – an earth so shallow that Merab is able to reach in and draw out the rabbit. Yet she has not always manifested these estimable qualities. While she underwent her obedience training without a hitch – she was neither exeptionally slow nor particularly adept during her basic training – when she first encountered rabbits she behaved so irrationally I believed she was mentally retarded. Only when I began to understand her ways did I realise what a priceless animal she was. I have never owned her equal, indeed, I have never seen her equal as a ferreter's dog. I often pity the chop and change dog owners that are so common amongst the lurcher fraternity. These people must acquire and pass on potentially valuable and useful dogs simply because they failed to understand the peculiarities the dogs possessed. There are no rapid methods of teaching a dog to mark inhabited holes – and most ferreters' dogs are two years of age before they can be classed as competent at the art of working with a ferret.

I break lurchers to ferret while they are still very young – indeed I often encourage a litter of puppies to play with safe, tame and reliable ferrets. My attention to familiarising lurchers to ferrets is, I believe, often criticised by some, but I take great pains to allow lurcher puppies to realise ferrets are allies. Frankly, I detest taking hunters on ferreting forays when, if asked if their lurchers are steady with ferrets they reply, 'I'm sure he'll be okay with ferrets', even though the dog eyes my ferrets with excited curiosity. Dogs aren't automatically steady with ferrets, they need to be convinced that ferrets aren't fair game and shouldn't be chased or harassed. If I am hunting with an associate who has a dog I believe to be unsteady with ferrets I leave all my dogs, puppies and adults alike, at home. Nothing is more infectious than stock worrying and I believe that even an oldstager, a longtime ferreter's dog, becomes less steady when it sees another dog harassing or killing a ferret – and ferrets die so easily when bitten by a dog. A puppy which witnesses the death of a ferret always regards ferrets with an unwholesome interest even after the mishap – and I never again trust a puppy that has joined in a worry. I dislike taking men, who have just bought 'the best dog you've ever seen' from some other temporary enthusiast, on a ferreting trip. The chances are that the wonder-dog just purchased will have been slipped at hare or run on the lamp and received no formal training or stock breaking.

Another pet hate is the man who insists on his dog checking every warren the handler sees. They bleat, 'Check here, check there!', and the dog responds by marking each and every hole whether it is inhabited or not. I can imagine no more destructive practice and the sight of a man urging his dog to check every hole really sets my teeth on edge. Dogs have to please their owners and eventually will start scratching at each and every hole just to please. A tale will illustrate my point. Some years ago David Hancock and I went ferreting with a young man who nearly drove both of us insane by the end of the day. He constantly spoke to his dog, to come to him, to go from him and to check every hole on the land we hunted. Three or four times the dog marked a hole, but Fathom who was a shade over the top speed-wise, but a magnificent hunter, simply ignored the dog that dug frantically at certain holes while the owner praised the dog's efforts. The young man chided Fathom's lack of marking ability when she ignored the dog, and then criticised my ferrets when they failed to bolt rabbits from the burrows his dog had marked. When Fathom marked my ferrets always found in the burrow, yet the young man still failed to appreciate that, by his constant bleating for the dog to check each hole, he was encouraging the dog to false mark.

Once a dog is used to being fixed or frozen above or near a burrow I allow the animal a certain amount of latitude obedience-wise, not a lot and certainly not enough to allow the dog to run amuck or seek out other holes, but enough to allow the dog to work out where to station itself at a vantage point to prepare to intercept the bolting rabbit. My best ferreting bitch, Merab, is allowed great latitude when working with ferrets though during her early training she needed a firm hand to control her. However, to maintain this firm hand relationship would have been counter-productive particularly as I regularly worked her with ferrets without netting up the burrows. It is amazing how may rabbits are held at the mouth of burrows by ferrets, ferrets that slowly draw the rabbit back into the burrow to kill it. Merab developed a technique of tensing her hind leg muscles and springing into the earths, seizing the rabbit and attached ferret and drawing both from the earth. She took several hundred rabbits this way.

Many lurchers become so intent on the struggles of the rabbit with the ferret taking place below the lurcher's feet that they are able to pinpoint where the ferret has killed its victim and allow the ferreter to dig to the kill. I have owned two bitches which could perform this feat with any degree of accuracy and both were from the same family, but one hears of spaniels, terriers and also collies that are also able to perform this feat with great accuracy. I know of no way of teaching this skill and firmly believe some dogs have a natural propensity to display this quality and that it cannot be taught the animal. Merab will always mark kills, yet her granddaughter, almost a replica of the older dog and nearly identically bred, – I am a confirmed line breeder – shows no inclination to mark kills below ground, despite the fact she will do virtually anything to please me and tries so hard to understand what I am trying to teach her.

My own personal opinion is that a warrener or full-time rabbiter would do well not to net every warren throughout the season and allow rabbits to run free and the lurcher to chase the bolting coneys. My reason for this notion is that dogs need to experience some satisfaction from any peculiarities they display if those peculiarities are to be continued and improved to the benefit of the hunting partnership. A dog that marks a warren, sees its owner/handler net up the warren, and a rabbit driven into the nets by the ferret – a rabbit which, incidentally, the lurcher must consider verboten and must be restrained from touching – must gain little pleasure from the process of marking an inhabited burrow and, hence, the tendency to mark inhabited burrows may diminish slightly as the season progresses. A burrow left unnetted, a rabbit allowed to bolt and the dog allowed to chase the rabbit gives a spiritual shot in the arm to the lurcher that is usually required to mark inhabited burrows but not to seize the netted rabbits.

On the subject of stopping lurchers mouthing netted rabbits, few lurchers cannot be restrained from this practice which is so destructive to carcase and purse net alike. Why teaching a lurcher to refrain from touching rabbits (few will refrain from touching rabbits of any sort) that are tangled in the nets is so simply taught is explained by the fact that when a rabbit strikes a net, causing it to purse on the rabbit, the coney ceases to struggle, partly because the meshes of the net restrict its movements and partly because rabbits that are frightened often freeze in an attempt to avoid capture. Dogs are often reluctant to attack an immobile rabbit (the subject of squatters will be dealt with in the chapter on lamping). Hence a verbal chastisement is often all that is necessary to prevent a dog mouthing a netted rabbit. It should, however, be added that once another dog joins the ferreting team it is by no means uncommon to find an otherwise net-steady dog mouthing netted rabbits. Lurchers are not of the right disposition to work alongside other dogs and the presence of another dog, even a well-behaved kennelmate, will cause a lurcher to react jealously.

I am often condemned for over-training a ferreting dog, for being a tyrannical martinet during the training programme in fact. I insist on netted rabbits being left strictly alone (I detest working a lurcher with another dog) but I allow a dog a chance to chase a rabbit that has slipped the folds of the net and is escaping. Once, and only once, has my insistence on rigid training methods come to grief. During Merab's early training she was taught that a free running rabbit was fair game but a netted one was verboten. One day in Strathy a rabbit hit the net, pulled the peg and continued hopping encased in the folds of the net. Free running rabbits were fair game, netted rabbits were forbidden. Now, however, a netted rabbit that was actually running away confronted Merab. The bitch's face took on the expression of bewilderment and she promptly fouled herself but recovered her composure enough to trap the rabbit with her feet.

She has never been put in a situation where she had to make such a momentous decision again, I should add, and is now a joy to own – an animal I will find virtually impossible to replace.

To train a ferreter's dog of any breed is no mean feat and is a lengthy and difficult process. No one is likely to sell a fully trained ferreter's dog, partly because the training of such an animal takes such a long time and partly because a ferreter's dog, an animal that has been trained to the standards just described, can keep a moucher in rabbits for many years and is such a priceless animal, few countrymen would wish to part with the dog. It is also worth noting that while a coursing dog, or rather, a lurcher kept exclusively for coursing, is a spent force by its seventh year – 'But when it has come to its seventh year, get it to a tanner' – the ferreter's lurcher will give useful service until its death. I ferreted with my lurcher bitch Fathom long after her eyesight began to fade and yet she never once false marked. No doubt I would still be using her today had not her descendant, Merab, become such an incredibly versatile animal. I have in fact never seen a 100 per cent ferreter's dog offered for sale.

12

Lamping

Lampers are attributed with a totally unjustified mystique by the majority of the lurcher and long dog world. They are credited with being all-seeing, all-knowing denizens of the darkness, as mystical as the darkness itself or mercurial as the starlight, a person as integral a part of the night as the darkness itself. Hokum, pure, ridiculous, unsubstantiated hokum! Next to the art of taking out a dog, lead-breaking it and slipping the dog at a hare or rabbit, teaching a dog the rudiments of lamping is the most simple of skills a lurcher enthusiast can learn. Most beginners to lurcher work start out by teaching their lurchers or long dogs to lamp. In fact, most sighthounds, indeed, most agile and swift breeds of dog, are capable of catching rabbits and hares when aided by a lamp.

Early books concerned with the exploits of poachers, most of which over glamourise the art of poaching until the seedy felons of the tales emerge as folk heroes, mention the taking of game, primarily partridge, by dint of the use of artificial light. This practice should not be confused with the activity known today as lamping, or spotlighting as the sport is known in Scotland. *Confessions Of A Poacher* mentions that dogs were trained to carry a lighted lantern suspended from their collars and this device apparently mesmerised partridge coveys so that the dog was able to snap up one or two birds or drive the bewildered covey towards a net set to entrap them. To date I have met no one who uses this method and when I experimented with this technique, making the ever-patient Fathom carry a lantern similar to the ones described in *Confessions of a Poacher* I achieved no success with this method, despite the fact that Fathom showed a great interest in hunting feather and that the owner of the land on which I worked was so enthusiastic about seeing the method used that he allowed me to work the fields for nearly two months. Perhaps I am not capable of teaching a dog to perform the said skill or perhaps the method is simply a 'drive the fool further' suggestion by the writer, and poaching books bristle with such silly stories.

The earliest reference to lamping forays I can find date to 1905, when cars with outlandish headlamps were stationed around a rabbit infested pasture, the car engines started, the fields floodlit and dogs of various types run at the bewildered rabbits. Just prior to my leaving Lichfield I watched a Landrover with a handler and his lurcher perched on the bonnet drive around the fields and at the appropriate time the lurcher, and a whippet concealed within the cab of the Landrover, were slipped at the rabbits. I'm sure the participants found the game exciting and some rabbits were certainly caught, but to compare the venture to a properly conducted lamping expedition would be ridiculous. The noise of the engine, the cries of the participants and, fault of faults, the barking of the excited dogs was scarcely conducive to efficient hunting, though it would be a lie to state that I did not find the spectacle entertaining and exciting.

My earliest lamping trips were conducted shortly after World War II when I watched a local eccentric, enormous lorry battery strapped to his back, shine a car headlamp attached to the battery, light up a field and run a rather collie-like lurcher at the rabbits illuminated by the beam of light. The weight of the heavy-duty ex-W.D. lorry battery was colossal and tale has it that the local eccentric went to his death toting the battery and lamp around the fields of a somewhat less than tolerant farmer who chased the lamper. The excitement, the exertion and the terrible weight of the battery brought about the demise of the lamper who, legend has it, sold his life for a trio of rabbits. Truly birthright sold for a mess of pot age!

Later more efficient, lighter batteries, batteries designed for use on motorbikes and motor scooters made life more bearable for the lamper and the quartz halide spotlamp also came as a godsend to him. By attaching this quartz halide lamp to the battery with a make and break circuit switch the lamper was able to shine his powerful beam of light and instantly shut off the light when he required the field to revert to its former darkness. These improvements caused a new type of moucher to evolve, a moucher who, by dint of lamp and lurcher, could net a haul of swag that would have taxed even the efforts of the Waltham Blacks – a fearsome nineteenth century band of professional poachers.

Lamping opened up new vistas for the moucher/poacher and while the practice of shining a brilliant light around a field to illuminate rabbits must seem a dangerous method of poaching game, the spate of convictions of unauthorised lampers during the 1970s gave no indication of how widespread lamping was. In the early 1970s magistrates treated the lamper as a joke, a harmless lunatic who shone lights around a field, more of a pest than a poacher. 'More of a voyeur than a villain' one magistrate described a lamper whose defence was he had yet to see a bull mate a cow and was observing the behaviour of the herd lit up by his lamp, but during the 1970s, the Golden Age of lamping perhaps, countless head of rabbit, hare and deer were killed by lamp and lurcher.

Shortly after the Lambourn lurcher show alerted the fieldsport authorities to the number of lurchers being bred and worked in Britain a spate of atrocities were attributed to the antics of lampers. Sheep were brought down, deer massacred in astounding numbers – the famous Leighton Buzzard poacher Geoffrey Battans pleaded to killing 201 deer with a lamp and a GSD-bred lurcher – Battans apparently killed several Pere David deer, a species extinct in the wild for 3,000 years. Battans' notoriety was short-lived however, for the famous Attingham Park slaughter, for such was the way the newspapers described the event, eclipsed the deeds of the Leighton Buzzard deer poacher. A band of three lurchermen entered Attingham Park near Shrewsbury and slew a number of fallow deer – the band were sentenced to eighteen months apiece and the lamper suddenly became Public Enemy Number One amongst gamekeepers and landowners alike. Henceforth, the sight of a beam of light shining around a field brought out estate watchmen, gamekeepers and police officers alike to investigate the source of the light. Henceforth lampers were seldom stopped, warned and told to go on their way, but prosecuted and sentenced by magistrates who rapidly became aware of how common the lamp-carrying poacher had become.

Yet the art of catching rabbits or hares with a lurcher aided by a beam of light is not illegal, providing, that is, that the lamper has a legal right to be on the land he is lamping. Police officers are seldom au fait with the laws concerning lamping – indeed one police superintendent declared that the practice was illegal – and in

1990 the national newspapers made great jest at this senior officer's ignorance of the law. Small wonder young police constables stop solitary lampers who are going about their lawful business and warn the said lampers of the prosecutions that await those who shine a beam of light around a field. Yet lamping is perfectly legal except in a few exceptional cases.

It is illegal to lamp deer – indeed it is illegal to chase and kill deer with dogs in Scotland. In England the hunter is committing an offence (even if he has permission to hunt on the land) if he kills or takes a deer one hour after darkness (lighting up time) and throughout the night until one hour before sunrise (Deer Act 1963 Section 2). Thus the deer should be considered forbidden quarry by the lamper, though more deer are killed by illegal lamping than by legitimate stalking so it appears, for the deer lamper observes no closed season (see later chapter).

I would advise any lamper who is starting out to learn the skills involved to use a Heath Robinson kit made from scrapyard pieces until he has mastered the technique of lamping and maintaining expensive equipment. My own lamping kit is a simple one and consists of a secondhand motorcycle battery which produces a beam of light from a quartz halide spot lamp – also obtained from a scrapyard. A Heath Robinson lightswitch enables me to switch the light off and on and the whole kit cost me about £6.00. When I first started lamping I carried an unbuffered battery in an ex-W.D. sidepack but within days acid spillage had perforated my carrier and corroded my jeans until they placed me in danger of committing indecency offences if I was apprehended during a night's lamping. After a while I cut down a gallon plastic container and placed the battery in this container, buffering the gap between battery and container with rolled up newspaper. The device looks awful and I feel embarrassed when I meet young lampers with Johnson and Johnson super-duper lamping kits, but the advantages of my own kit are many.

Firstly, if any portion of my kit is damaged it can easily be replaced by a trip to the scrapyard – batteries, headlamps, wires and even plastic containers have been replaced over the years. Furthermore, I am extremely remiss about maintaining electrical or mechanical equipment and hence my lamp kit suffers badly through misuse. Add to this the fact that I am also remarkably clumsy and damage to my kit is frequent. A good class kit of the sort Johnson and Johnson of Sheffield sell would, I am afraid, be a little wasted on someone like me. Conversely, my equipment has been known to be defective from time to time – indeed at one time my associates stated that the novel 'The Light That Failed' was a tale of my lamping adventures! Likewise, so poor is my technical expertise there have been times when the light has flashed on without my touching the switch. Lamping with such devices is quite cheap but very inefficient.

Some of the modern lamping kits, often advertised rather ironically in view of their use as security lamps, are truly wonderful affairs, virtually foolproof and so well made as to be almost indestructable. Some emit such a powerful beam of light that they might light up a field a mile distant or illuminate a whole field with an almost blinding light – a far cry from any ill-fitting quartz halide beam and a motorbike battery in my possession.

The majority of poachers arrested by police seldom use these elaborate high powered beams. Most rely on adapted quartz halide lamps, the circumference of which is painted black so that only a narrow beam of light escapes from the lamp. Poachers argue that a fine beam of light flickering around a field attracts less attention than a full beam. Frankly I feel that is illogical. A powerful headlight shining around a field might be mistaken for the headlamp of a motorcycle parked or reversing out of a gateway. A pencil-thin light flickering almost eerily around the centre of fields is sure to attract attention. It can be argued that rabbits all too easily move out of the pencil-thin beam and can be lost in the darkness. Likewise, a more powerful beam will not only illuminate the rabbit but also the pitfalls and dangers of the field. I have never favoured pencil-thin beams and have yet to see one used to good effect.

When poachers started using lamps to capture rabbits, hares and partridge their capers were considered extremely daring by the sporting fraternity. In point of fact, the lamper was, at that time at least, seldom in serious danger of detection from either police or gamekeepers. A lamper stationed behind the beam is virtually invisible to the investigator approaching him. If the officer approached the poacher, the light of the beam almost blinded anyone facing the beam and once the light was switched off the poacher could invariably vanish into the blackness and escape detection. Furthermore, most lampers choose to venture abroad in pitch black nights made more unpleasant still by high wind and driving rain. Police officers too have human frailties and were seldom enthusiastic about seeking out an eccentric shining a light around a muddy field, particularly if the apprehended poacher received only a mild rebuke from magistrates when the poacher was taken to task by the police. At first when lamping became a popular method of poaching, gamekeepers and police alike were baffled with how to contend with the lamper. Today, however, it is a very different matter for both police and gamekeepers are now well trained to cope with the apprehension of lamp-carrying poachers.

Police and gamekeepers alike now carry very high-powered lamps and seldom venture into fields to apprehend the poachers. Keepers and police alike will wander the lanes near the estate where lampers are operating and seek out parked cars. Poachers returning to their cars, with or without the swag (for many secrete the game to pick up at a later time in the evening) will then need to explain their activities to the officers waiting near the cars. Very few poachers are actually apprehended in the act of taking rabbits and hares. Most are arrested as they return to their cars or are being picked up by accomplices who are around the estate waiting for the lamper to appear at some entrance to a field. The image of the Robin Hood figure, an image enjoyed by the poacher since the Norman Conquest, is a ludicrous one and totally false. There are few cases of poachers ever running the gauntlet of police and gamekeepers in order to obtain food to feed a starving family. The majority of poachers and mouchers alike poach in order to indulge in a spot of excitement, the consequences of capture are today seldom severe anyway. Genuine poachers, rather than mouchers (the differences have been explained), who strike at the heart of the game estate and denude the said estate of all saleable game are simply criminals who are indulging in yet another aspect of criminal behaviour. In 1985 I conducted a survey concerning the convictions of persons who were found guilty of poaching. The moucher type, invader of farms and shoots, were simply freelancers, often otherwise respectable men, out to catch a rabbit or two for sport and excitement. Dyed-in-the-wool genuine poachers were invariably unemployed (often through choice) and had a criminal record that indicated that they were also adept at many other types of theft. The courts were obviously able to distinguish the difference between mouchers and poachers and sentenced accordingly.

The act of lamping rabbits and hares however is perfectly legal, providing one has permission to be lamping on the land one is hunting. Certain nights are more suitable for lamping however. A bright, moonlit night might be a pleasant night to walk abroad but such a night is usually singularly unproductive regarding the capture of rabbits and hares. On such nights rabbits and hares are usually able to watch the lamping party approach and take flight long before the dogs are able to be slipped or run at the quarry. Ideal lamping nights are all too rare even in a country with the climate of Britain. The perfect night for lamping should be:

a) inky black;
b) windy – but not too windy;
c) with some drizzle perhaps – but not a night accompanied by lashing rain;
d) a night when the ground is not frozen solid;
e) a night which is not illuminated by lights other than the lamper's beam.

Inky-black, moonless nights occur perhaps three or four nights a month during wintertime, and no lamper should be abroad in spring or summertime when rabbits and hares are breeding. On nights such as this a lamper and his dog can approach to within a dozen yards of the feeding rabbit without alerting the creature. The sound of footfall is, in fact, the only method the rabbit has of detecting the presence of a predator of any sort on such a night.

If the night is not only raven's wing black, but also windy then the rabbit or hare is at an even greater disadvantage for the scent of man – and human beings are, according to Denbeck, incredibly smelly creatures – is dispersed by the wind and the noise of footfall reduced by the sound of the said wind. Such nights are absolutely ideal for lamping and, barring accidents these are the nights when a lamper will not only secure his greatest hauls but also his easiest catches. On nights such as these lampers can often approach the rabbit so closely as to be able to stoop and pick up the squatting coney, particularly if the land on which the rabbits are feeding has not been lamped before – rabbits are not as stupid as zoologists would have hunters believe and learn from unpleasant experiences.

Too strong a wind – a gale such as Caithness experienced in January of 1988 – constitutes far from ideal lamping weather. When strong winds of this force occur broken branches and certain objects are blown around the fields, few animals, herbivores and predators alike, will venture abroad to feed in these conditions. At the time of the gale I ventured forth, lamp in hand, to batten down a pig ark that was rolling around the field trapped in the grip of a gust from the north and I noticed that the fields near my pigpen which were usually thick with rabbits at that time were deserted, though I came on a grounded tawny owl in the deep, dead-thistle beds.

I've started the tale so I'll finish it. I reached down to lift the owl, which despite its bruised and battered condition footed my hand with its talons. Tales of Eric Hoskin came to mind and as I am not a brave man I left the owl to its own devices. Three days later the storm had not abated and the owl still remained crouched in the thistle bed but was gone as soon as the storm blew itself out.

Various birds are grounded by strong winds, however, and lampers often find their dogs picking up pheasants that have been blown down by gales. In coastal regions fulmars are often unable to fly when blown down by strong winds, but lurchers and sighthounds alike give these strange gull-like birds a clear berth. Fulmars that are unable to fly after a bad battering from storms regurgitate a strong fishy fluid which they spit at dogs. This oily fluid is corrosive and painful to the eyes and hence few dogs will seek to carry a downed fulmar to the lamper. Tales of dogs refusing to approach such a gull are legion.

Some drizzle carried on the wind helps deaden the sound of the lamper approaching a rabbit or hare but a heavy downpour is not conducive to lamping forays. Rabbits will not venture out in heavy rain unless, that is, the rain lasts for several days as it did in three successive winters in the 1970s, when hunger forced rabbits to feed in blinding rain. Hares are somehow able to find safe havens above ground in such conditions and are seldom seen by lampers enthusiastic enough to venture out and face the elements. Gamebirds such as partridge will at times become so wet as to be unable to fly, though such birds are usually sick or wounded, for the carefully placed plumage of the partridge is usually weatherproof enough to prevent the filoplume becoming saturated. Nevertheless, partridge and pheasants are sometimes caught by lurchers after constant, heavy downpours of rain.

I have many times ventured out in heavy rain, gales and even bad sleet to catch rabbits to feed ferrets or puppies, but I draw the line at running any dog when the temperature drops low enough to freeze the land. A fall on such land, even a slight fall, can be injurious and painful to the dog but worse still frost ridges that pucker the soil when the temperatures remain below zero for several days rip pads and wrists alike when a dog passes over these ridges. The damage wrought by running a dog over frost ridges often defies belief and once a dog is badly damaged it is hors de combat for the rest of the season. The problem is that despite the fact that lurchers are delightfully placid animals they will often continue to pursue quarry even after they are bloody, broken and racked with pain. Dogs will often work until the end of the night before the lamper discovers that the dog has received a huge rip that should have incapacitated the lurcher at the moment the rip was inflicted. The desire to hunt quarry often masks the most hideous of hurts. In the winter of 1981 Gerald Barlow, a landowner from Whittington, was greatly troubled by poachers, or mouchers who are nuisances rather than thieves. One morning while waiting to go to work I walked one of my lurchers up by his gateway over ground frozen so hard that a fall would have done a dog great damage. Bloody footprints led across Barlow's field, footprints that indicated that a dog had severed the central pad to produce such a quantity of gore. Yet the trail indicated that the lamper had stopped twice to lamp rabbits and the dog had obviously run to catch the coneys. The lurcher must have endured intense agony when walking, let alone running, but it had probably endured the pain without complaint and gone on to finish the night's work. A dog so injured would not have run again that season and in all probability would have climbed aboard the carousel of Midland dog dealers.

The conditions of Section (e) must cause the tyro dog trainer a great deal of confusion but the fact is that many areas are so illuminated by the orange glow of street lights as to be too light to lamp well. As I write I gaze across the Pentland Firth and the street lights of Kirkwall have suffused the skyline with an orange glow. Kirkwall is a tiny town with a population of some six thousand or so people but the street lights are visible some twenty miles away. Thurso, population 8,000, some sixteen miles from my home now illuminates the skyline as would a Bessemer blast furnace. Now, rabbits quite often live in pockets of wasteland within the town and the permanent daylight afforded by street lamps must make these rabbits extremely shy to lamp. Yet, ironically, lurchers are more numerous in the building estates surrounding large towns than they are in the tiny villages in the countryside.

The basic training that should precede the entering of a lamp dog should, if anything, be more stringent than even the training given to a ferreter's dog or a daytime lurcher. A recalcitrant, difficult dog that is reluctant to return to hand is a problem during daylight hours. When such a dog decides to behave badly in darkness the problem becomes nightmarish. A loose dog dashing hither and thither putting feeding rabbits to ground and a handler desperately calling the dog to hand is certainly not a desirable combination. A lamping dog must be a dog that is under control from the moment it leaves the house until it returns. However, many of the dogs offered for sale as competent lampers are far from obedient and well-trained, for just as no one seems willing to sell a ferreting dog, likewise the first-class lamper, the obedient dog that fetches instantly to hand, returns at the click of the handler's fingers and runs only when required to do so seldom sees the inside of a dealer's kennel.

However, it would be impossible to leave the subject of basic training without mention of the subject of teaching the lamping dog to jump, or rather whether a lamping dog should ever be taught to jump. Many believe that to teach a lamping dog to jump is to court disaster as a dog that shows an inclination to jump will leap fences in total darkness and land on wire, farm machinery or topple into an abyss-like quarry. Many, many lamp dogs are killed in this manner. My own competitive jumping dog met his death in this way. However it should also be pointed out that a great many dogs come to grief during daytime coursing forays – and a non-jumping dog is of little use as a courser. However, the sight of people lifting a large, healthy dog over fences, hedges, stiles and gates looks ridiculous particularly if the said handler is also encumbered by his lamping kit and a backpack full of rabbits. Personally I have never seen the logic of not teaching a lamping dog to jump. A non-jumping dog is of little use as a daytime courser, of very little use as a ferreter's dog and a damned heavy object to lift over gates and fences at night. I own two lamping/ferreting/daytime lurchers both of which jump well.

No lamp dog should ever be entered to quarry before it is well and truly trained and sound in both wind and limb. The process of trying a young puppy at a lamped rabbit – a so-called 'easy' rabbit (and I have heard of even twelve-week old puppies being subjected to this type of entering) – is both ludicrous and ruinous. A whelp is not only strained by a course against an animal that can out-match it, but becomes a defeated down-spirited lurcher if its efforts are not rewarded by a catch. The vice of opening up, of barking, is born from such a practice – and the subject of opening up will be dealt with presently. Few lurchers are well enough trained to enter to lamped quarry before they are a year old and personally I feel a good eighteen months of training is needed before a puppy is obedient enough to be taken on a lamping trip.

How a puppy should be entered to lamping is often hotly debated by lurchermen. Certainly a lurcher puppy is usually less over-matched by a lamped rabbit than it would be by the same rabbit run during the daylight hours. Rabbits seldom feed far from their burrows during daylight hours – a few yards at the most, but under the cover of darkness they venture abroad some hundred or so yards to feed. A lurcher, particularly a large lurcher or match bred long dog, is seldom able to generate enough instant speed to catch a rabbit feeding only yards from its burrow, but a lurcher has a far better chance of gathering enough speed to catch a rabbit that has to run a hundred or so yards to find sanctuary. For this reason lurchers and long dogs are often entered or 'started' at lamped rabbits long before they are allowed to pursue a rabbit during daylight hours.

If the lamper has a competent, sound and steady lamp dog available, entering a puppy, or rather, sapling, to the lamp is simplicity itself. If the puppy is taken out on a slip and held while a mature dog runs and possibly catches a rabbit, the youngster soon associates the beam of light with the appearance of a rabbit in the beam. Lamping simply involves the lurcher or long dog associating the beam of light with the beam illuminating the quarry the lurcher is required to run. Once the puppy realises it must watch the beam of light its training is virtually complete – though it takes some time for a lurcher to polish its act, so to speak. However, this method of entering is not without its problems – and frankly it is a method I dislike intensely.

A competent, reliable lamping dog run at a rabbit with the handler holding a young dog behind the lamp – a young dog that is likely to pull towards the lurcher carrying the rabbit or, worse still, snatch at the rabbit, soon becomes a bad retriever or a reluctant retriever which circles the handler unwilling to give up its catch to the handler lest the other dog seizes its prize. A lamp dog that circles, catch in mouth, is one of the most annoying of animals, but this peculiarity is seldom the result of an innate disposition, but is a malaise brought about by working two or more dogs together. More lamping dogs are ruined by stationing another dog behind the beam than by any other training malpractice. My own strain of lurcher is inordinately jealous of working in the presence of another dog be the hunt conducted in daylight or at night and frankly this method of entering just described would have a ruinous effect on the performance of my seasoned, experienced lurchers.

If a seasoned, experienced lamping dog is not available to assist the entering of a sapling lurcher all is certainly not lost – in fact there is considerable evidence to show that it is bad policy to allow a puppy to ape the technique of an older dog. Vices as well as virtues are in fact all too easily copied by puppies and saplings. I confess that I never use a lurcher to train another dog the knack of lamping and lamping is, quite simply, a knack that can be taught any fairly athletic breed of dog. I usually choose a night during which I intend to start a puppy very carefully, for, just as nothing succeeds like success so nothing daunts a sapling more than persistent failure. Thus, when a dark windy night occurs I take out my lurcher sapling and attempt to enter it to lamped rabbit. I choose the sapling's first rabbit with some care. I ignore rabbits that are sitting ears erect near hedges or warrens and I try to select a rabbit my puppy is not only able to run, but also, with luck, able to catch. My ideal rabbit is a sitter, a rabbit that is squatted, ears back, in the centre of a large field and it is this rabbit I shall encourage the puppy to catch. If only unsuitable rabbits present themselves on the night I do not slip the puppy but allow the lurcher to watch rabbits running illuminated by the beam, and if the sapling bucks and struggles as it stares down the beam so much the better, for I assume the lurcher has seen the rabbit. When, and only when, I find an ideally placed rabbit will I slip the puppy and do my utmost to keep the rabbit in the beam as the lurcher pursues it. If the lurcher succeeds in catching the rabbit I shut off the beam or shine the beam around me as I crouch to entice the puppy to come to hand carrying its catch.

It's a curious fact that puppies that have sickened of retrieving the dummy – any dummy, in fact, even the cadaver of a long dead rabbit – will often retrieve its catch to hand, or almost to hand. Most puppies return their first rabbit almost to hand and, elated by their catch, walk around the handler, rabbit carried high. The handler should not pursue the puppy to relieve it of its catch but simply squat until the whelp brings the rabbit either to hand or drops the rabbit at the handler's feet – and most puppies are so excited by their first catch that they seldom deliver to hand in the manner of a springer. In time, when the novelty of catching has lessened slightly, the whelp, if trained properly, will fetch its catch to hand. On no account, and I cannot stress this too strongly, should the handler bring along another dog when the puppy makes its first catch. Such practice is certain to start that most maddening of faults – circling – the lurcher, rabbit in mouth, circles the handler but refuses to give up its catch.

A point even some experienced lurchermen fail to note is that a young lurcher may well find the pursuit and capture of a rabbit running away from the dog fairly simple. However, young dogs find it very difficult to pick up or catch a rabbit that is running towards them. It is surprising how many young dogs seem bewildered when rabbits run directly at them – as lamped rabbits are wont to do when startled (particularly if the rabbits have never been lamped before – such as rabbits living on remote farms and rabbits at the beginning of the season). Ilan, my lurcher stud dog and sire of the best lurchers I've ever bred, was baffled when his first lamped rabbit ran towards him and leapt sideways to avoid collision with the rabbit. Ironically, his first three lamped rabbits ran towards him and I felt that he would never learn the technique of catching lamped rabbits. His fourth rabbit ran away from him and his enormous stride enabled him to overtake and catch the rabbit in a trice. He became an excellent lamper – he was faster than most of his ancestors or descendants – and caught rabbits at every conceivable angle until his accident rendered him crippled. All my lurchers are descended from him, he became, in fact, the scion of my strain and sire and grandsire of the best workers I've ever bred.

On the subject of squatting rabbits, many rabbits escape capture simply by the act of squatting when they are illuminated by the beam. Sapling hounds are often reluctant to seize rabbits when they are motionless and squatters often need to be made to run before the sapling lurcher will pursue them. Older dogs, in fact quite elderly lampers, often become so efficient at detecting the presence of squatting rabbits and seizing the rabbits before they start to run that it becomes profitable to keep these lurchers in active service rather than retire them. Fathom became extremely adept at picking up squatters until her seventeenth year for, despite her stiff, geriatric movement, she'd walk up to the squatting rabbits, gently seize them and return the rabbits equally gently to hand. She would ignore rabbits that were preparing to run and simply seek out those that sat ears back trying to escape detection.

Squatters are more common at the beginning of the season when as many as one in three rabbits will squat rather than attempt to run. However, while the technique works well at evading human beings and young lurchers, adult foxes and mature lurchers find squatters such easy meat that the proportion of squatters to running rabbits decreases rapidly as the season progresses. Less than one in six rabbits will be enthusiastic about squatting in the beam before the lamping season comes to an end. Rabbits that are lamped regularly – rabbits that survive the trauma of living near a large, lurcher-rich housing estate – seldom squat to escape capture but run for home as soon as a lamp flickers around the field. Rabbits that are educated to the beam – rabbits that run for home at the first sign of a light – are extremely difficult to lamp and I avoid taking my young lurchers to places that are regularly hunted by lampers. Rabbits that are used to being chased by a lurcher aided by a beam of light are usually more than a match for a young, inexperienced sapling.

To the tyro lurcherman or the hunter with little or no experience of the behaviour of rabbits, it would seem as though the sight of a beam flashing around a field, or the action of a dog chasing a rabbit, would automatically put every rabbit feeding in the same field to ground. In point of fact rabbits seldom feed in groups, not even when rabbit kittens are still suckling the doe. Lockley, author of *The Private Life of the Rabbit* believes that this curious behaviour could be due to the fact that rabbits are innately suspicious of one another. Another explanation of this peculiar behaviour seems more plausible, however. By avoiding group feeding behaviour, one or more of the litter will, or could, survive the concerted attack of a predator. This theory is countered by the fact that greylags and other species of geese feed in groups as a form of protection against predator attack – each member of the gaggle acts as a sentinel to alert the group to the presence of any form of danger. However, rabbits will seldom feed in groups and unless a field is lamped regularly the rest of the litter will continue to feed even though one of their number has been caught by a lurcher. As has been explained, however, once the field is regularly lamped rabbits high-tail it for home as soon as a beam of light flickers around the field.

Perhaps it is time to deal with the subject of the dog giving tongue while chasing, or 'opening up' as the vice is described in poaching parlance. This vice once reduced the value of a supposedly serviceable lurcher to practically zero. The majority of lurcherwork is conducted on land without the permission of the landowners and hence any dog that alerts the landowner to the presence of trespassers is a liability. A dog that barks, opens up or gives tongue while chasing is, therefore, a liability to the moucher-cum-poacher and many dogs are sold on because they manifest this vice. As to what causes opening up, there are many theories but before examining these theories and discussing their validity it is wise to examine the sequence of events that usually precede the dog starting to bark, open up or give tongue. A dog that is gaining on its grey and seems likely to catch the quarry usually runs silently and only when the quarry seems likely to escape does the dog start to give tongue. For instance, confirmed yappers will seldom make a sound when run at rabbits incapacitated with myxomatosis, yet bay like thunder when they chase a hare.

Several theories are offered concerning why a dog gives tongue when chasing, and once the problem starts it is virtually impossible to break the dog of the habit, one should add. Breeding is said to be one reason why a dog gives tongue while coursing. Certain breeds, certain crosses, are said to be particularly prone to open up when coursing. Whippets and whippet hybrids are said to be particularly prone to give tongue when running, though it has been said that whippets have acquired this reputation for being vocal simply because the din that precedes a whippet race is cacophonous and wouldbe mouchers considers that a din of this intensity would start to manifest itself in the field. Certainly whippet lurchers (as opposed to whippetbred long dogs) are sometimes prone to give tongue. I have always attributed this peculiarity to the fact that a whippet lurcher (a Bedlington, collie or another terrier/whippet hybrid) is a shade too small to come to terms with healthy, strong rabbits and the yelp is simply a cry for help as the quarry starts to escape. Strong, purebred or track bred (greyhound/whippet hybrids) whippets are usually large enough and fast enough to catch most rabbits and hence, are seldom as guilty of giving tongue as are the heavier, slower whippet lurchers.

My own personal opinion is that vocal lurchers or sighthounds are not born but made and I attribute nearly all cases of dogs opening up to premature entering or running a dog that is not fit enough or capable enough to catch its quarry. Perhaps I might explain the reason for my theory more fully and resort to an anecdote to prove a point. I bred a fairly inbred strain of lurcher, a collie-blooded mongrelised strain that now breeds true to type. Possibly due to the fact that I choose homes for my puppies carefully and advise against premature entering I have seldom produced lurchers with a tendency to opening up when coursing. However in 1990 I produced a lurcher with a great propensity to open up, though the animal had every reason to be vocal while coursing. Some time ago a puppy I had given to Bruce Warburton, an efficient Dornoch-based lurcherman, sustained an accident that resulted in the amputation of a left hind leg. The injury was horrific but Bruce kept the puppy which not only learned to balance on three legs, but coursed and caught rabbits. However, such was her disability that when a rabbit succeeds in outrunning her – a jinking rabbit is terribly difficult for a three-legged dog to catch – she emits a slight 'yip', a cry for help or a yelp of frustration.

It is interesting to note that despite her terrible disability the bitch has caught a great number of rabbits and also one hare – it would have been even more interesting to have seen how this animal would have hunted if it had kept all its limbs.

I would never advise any lurcherman to enter a puppy too soon or to deliberately over-match any lurcher, for I believe the seeds of opening up are born out of such a practice. Perhaps there are some dogs that have a natural propensity to open up when hunting, but I believe the vice is a result of nurture rather than nature and can be prevented. In passing it is worth noting that at one time terrier-blooded lurchers were said to be the main culprits regarding the vice of opening up. It should, however, also be mentioned that both Bedlington and Irish terriers (the most important terrier baselines used in lurcher breeding) have a reputation for being mute underground. Indeed the slightest yicker from an Irish terrier competing in the Teastas Mor (a test of courage involving facing a badger) meant the disqualification of the terrier.

On the subject of vices it must be said that one of the most serious problems a lurcherman may encounter is when his lurcher develops a tendency to kill or crush any rabbit it catches. Damaged carcases, carcases with punctured ribcages, bruised back muscles, are worth only a fraction of the value of undamaged rabbits. Hence the dog that manifests a hard mouth – a desire to catch and crunch rabbits – is worth considerably less than a soft mouthed dog.

It is possible – though, just possible – that hard mouthed dogs are the result of nature rather than nurture, but there is considerable evidence to suggest that dogs which show a natural inclination to carry live rabbits to hand can, under certain circumstances, develop a tendency to kill and bruise or puncture rabbits they catch and carry. Lurchers soon learn that it is easier to carry a corpse than a live, kicking coney. Thus, when dogs are run so often that they begin to tire, many will kill the rabbit they are carrying rather than exhaust themselves further carrying the rabbit live to hand. Thus, dogs that are run too hard and too often may well develop a hard mouth.

It is often said that dogs that are run too regularly on hare or fox develop hard mouths, and, indeed, it is exceedingly difficult for any dog to carry a live hare to hand and extremely dangerous to retrieve a live fox. Yet dogs that regularly catch and kill both foxes and hares are often exceedingly gentle when carrying a live rabbit. It appears as though the intensity of the struggle put up by the quarry may well determine its condition when the lurcher returns the catch to hand. Southerd's Lady, quite a famous match running dog in her day caught a great many hares yet retrieved rabbits live to hand. Likewise, some of the best fox catching dogs I have ever seen were so soft mouthed that they returned unharmed pheasant poults to hand.

Once a dog has developed a hard mouth there is nothing a lurcher handler can do to cure the complaint. Tales of cures being effected by encouraging a lurcher to retrieve a hedgehog or a rabbit wrapped in barbed wire should be ignored. Most dogs can learn the technique of carrying live hedgehogs and commanding a dog to fetch a rabbit wrapped in barbed wire is an almost certain method of stopping a dog retrieving to hand. There is nothing one can do to cure the malaise of hard mouth but I believe the problem can be prevented by not running a dog to a state where its exhaustion ensures it will kill the rabbit rather than carrying the still struggling coney to hand and never running an unfit dog at rabbits, for an unfit dog tires rapidly and, if it catches, kills its prey rather than carrying the kicking rabbit alive to hand.

A hot potato fieldsport subject is the lamping of the brown hare – that champion athlete – a quarry which during the daylight hours is a match for the fastest hound yet a reasonably easy quarry for even a second-rate lamping dog. Dogs which do not have the speed to turn a hare coursed during the daylight hours often bring down hares that are illuminated and baffled by the lamper's beam. At the time of writing there are fieldsport groups, including long dog aficionados, that are urging parliament to make the hunting of the hare with artificial lights (lamping devices) illegal; it should be remembered that it is already illegal to lamp deer. As to the morality of lamping hare, I will pass no comment except to say I have seldom owned a dog that was a match for a fair law daytime hare but I have lamped and, indeed, caught, many hares with my lurchers.

When a rabbit is illuminated in a beam it will either run for home or squat in the hope of escaping detection. The lamped hare will give of its best to escape capture, running at its fastest, but whereas the hare coursed during daylight hours runs cunningly using each and every obstacle to its advantage to escape its pursuer, the lamped hare runs madly, often turning back and running towards the lamper as if made bereft of its senses by the beam lighting its flight path. So panic-stricken does the hare become that I know of few lampers who cannot relate tales of lamped hare running into the lamper or of hares killed by a kick from the lamper as they pass by, lurcher in hot pursuit. Small wonder the coursing purists wish to see the lamping of hares made illegal!

Yet to assume that the pursuit of hares is easy meat for a lurcher, even a lurcher aided by a lamping device, is a mistake. A hare is a soul-destroying opponent for any dog and while it has to be conceded that a hare illuminated by a beam of light runs less cunningly and makes less use of the obstructions and terrain of the field in which it is coursed, the exertions required of the lurcher to bring such a hare to hand are terrific. Tyro lurchermen should treat tales of thirty hares caught by a single dog during a lamping foray with some care. Dogs of any breed are seldom capable of the effort of bringing down thirty hares – even thirty lamped hares during a night's lamping. A single run at a lamped hare will usually have the fittest lurcher panting, sides heaving and too winded to run for several minutes and three or four hares run that night will usually find the dog swaying with exhaustion or dead on the field. Landowners and keepers in the Cambridgeshire area often report finding dead lurchers in the middle of huge fields that are well-stocked with strong hares and there is every reason to believe these dogs have expired during lamping forays.

Lampers who seek to supplement their living by selling their wares, for no one can make even a small living by lamping – I have explained the economics of this in my books *In Pursuit of Coney* and *Sighthounds* – will often switch off the lamp and call in the dog when a hare leaps up in the beam. A dog will often exhaust itself in the pursuit of a single hare – a difficult to sell type of catch that will seldom fetch more than £2.50. Yet the same dog in fit condition, given some time to recover between runs will, in good rabbit country, at the start of a season when rabbits are plentiful, chase and catch as many as thirty rabbits during a night's lamping. A hare run at the start of a lamping foray will usually ensure the lurcher does not give of its best for the rest of the night, so the pursuit of hares with lamp and lurcher is not only a shade less sporting than daytime coursing but seldom financially worthwhile when rabbits are abundant.

Lampers are seldom aware that the hare, unlike the rabbit, is included in the definition of game and, hence, it is illegal to hunt or lamp hares on a Sunday or Christmas Day. It should also be noted that hares, once again unlike rabbits, are afforded some protection during their breeding season. Sections 2 and 3 of the Hares Preservation Act of 1892 makes it an offence to sell or offer for sale any hare or leveret between the months of March and July, though in dry years hares will often produce leverets in early September. What is not realised by the majority of lampers is that it is an offence under Section 23 of the Game Act of 1831 to seek out and kill hares without the lamper being in possession of a game certificate – hares are classed as game, rabbits are not. It is of interest perhaps to note that members of the Royal Family would not require a game licence should they wish to lamp hares (Game Licence Act 1960).

I am often asked which types of lurcher make the best lampers and though I have tried so hard not to be seen to promote the collie lurcher throughout this book, I can say the very best lamp dogs I have ever seen have been collie bred lurchers or lurchers that had a strong trace of collie in their ancestry. The size of the dog, however, is nearly as important as the breeding of the lamping dog. I freely admit I have seen deerhound-sized lurchers, dogs of thirty or thirty-one inches at the shoulder display wonderful dexterity at picking up lamped rabbits or hares, but to suggest that this size of dog was ideal would be inaccurate and ludicrous.

Smaller dogs are much more suited to the nip and tuck sport of lamping. Such dogs are able to hit top speed in a matter of a second or so (a larger lurcher takes time to gain impetus), change direction in a stride and are seldom as accident-prone as larger, more powerfully built dogs. If asked for the ideal size for the lamping lurcher or, indeed, for the all-round moucher's lurcher, I would say between twenty-three and twenty-four and a half inches. Smaller dogs have to try so much harder to catch their quarry, while larger, more powerful dogs, though they may be devastatingly efficient at catching hares granted fair law, are seldom agile enough to work in places where rabbits are usually abundant – fields or wasteland where rubble, steep banks or gorse patches are common.

I cannot resist debunking silly superstitions concerned with lamping. At one time it was virtually impossible to sell a pied lurcher, particularly a gay pied (with more white than base colour) as a lamping dog and such coloured puppies were often put down at birth. The theory was that most lampers hunted in places where they were unwelcome and here a pied dog would be far more conspicuous than dark-coloured or brindle dogs (though straw-coloured Norfolk lurchers were supposedly not conspicuous). I ask the reader to consider the facts – what would be more conspicuous, what indeed could attract more attention from a hostile landowner, than the sight of a beam of light shining around a field in the pitch darkness of a moonless night. White dogs, pied dogs and straw-coloured dogs with satinised coats (each hair follicle is transparent) would pass unnoticed by the landowner once a field was illuminated by a beam of light. Lampers are seldom logical people, so it would seem.

Certain lampers swear by certain techniques to assist their dogs in the catching of rabbits and hares. Most believe, and I confess I use the technique myself, that if a beam of light is allowed to flicker on a hedge through which a hare or rabbit is attempting to run, the process is often referred to as 'rocking the lamp', the quarry is delayed a second or so – perhaps it is startled by the flickering light and this affords the lurcher a better chance of catching the rabbit or hare. It is also commonly believed that if a hare runs through a hedge the lamper should continue to shine the lamp on the hedge as the hare is almost certain to return to the field from which it has escaped the attentions of the lamper. Hares tend to run circuitous routes and are often quite likely to return to the same field where a dog has chased them. It must be mentioned that rocking the lamp is not an infallible method of delaying the flight of the rabbit, particularly if the rabbit has been lamped before. Rabbits that are regularly harassed by lampers are decidedly suspicious of lamp beams and seldom give a lurcher a chance to come to terms with them. Likewise no hare is instinctively obliged to come back through the fence to face the lamper.

There is, however, one infallible rule that will, if observed, help the lamper make better hauls of rabbits and hares. The lamper must develop a symbiotic relationship with his lurcher. He must know his lurcher's peculiarities and the lurcher must understand, or at least tolerate, the idiosyncrasies of the lamper. The constant chopping and changing of lurchers affords the lurcher keeper little chance to really understand the animal he is working, for he has little time to develop a relationship with the lurcher. A lurcher should be a dog for life, a long-term investment, not simply a dog bought for the winter and passed on when the rabbiting season comes to an end.

Equally important to success at lamping is the fact that the efficient lamper must forego any attempt to join the lamping parties that wander the countryside after dark. These parties are ruinous to the discipline and efficiency of the dog. Often two dogs are slipped at the same rabbit and collisions are often extremely injurious to the dogs that run into each other at top speed. Lurcherman vies with lurcherman for the title of 'Owner of the Best Dog' and young dogs develop bad habits when taken on such trips. Retrieving suffers most when a dog is required to bring a catch to hand while a dozen or so other dogs lunge and snatch at the catch. When I give a puppy to a friend I always tell the owner of the jealous nature of my own strain: they simply will not perform when another dog is present, rather they develop retrieving vices if another dog looks like snatching their catch. My own strain of lurcher is the most jealous retriever imaginable and I will not work them while other dogs are present. If I receive lurcher-owning visitors I do not hesitate to offend when the owner prepares me for the almost inevitable question, 'Is it alright if I bring Ben along?' My reply is always that if he brings Ben along my own dogs stay at home. I hate chaos and the sight of a pack of unruly lurchers sets my teeth on edge. After many years of experience of lurchers and the people who keep them I have come to the conclusion that despite their garishly masculine appearance many lampers are afraid of venturing out after dark. Lamping is a one man, one dog activity and the crowds who accompany a lamping party are out of place and counter-productive to a night's hunting. It is legally permissible to hunt rabbits summer and winter alike with no regard to the breeding season of the species, for the rabbit, unlike the hare, is afforded no protection by law. It is, however, morally irresponsible to continue to hunt rabbits once the first signs of breeding are observed. I seldom wait to catch a pregnant doe before I finish hunting. When I observe buck scut, fur stripped from rabbits during the conflict of bucks determining dominance as does come into season, I stop lamping, ferreting and netting. It is grossly unfair to kill does that have youngsters in the nest and certainly does not help conserve a healthy breeding stock for the next season. I begin hunting when the first frosts start to wither the sow thistle in the district, a sign I take as an indication that no more rabbit kits will be born that season. To hunt rabbits during the summer months – a time when does are carrying and suckling young kittens is not only counter-productive to obtaining a good haul of rabbits the following winter but unfair and unsporting.

The duration of the active life of a lamping dog is the subject of much debate amongst lurcher buffs. Many lurchers are retired and sold on long before their seventh season. Few lurchers are afforded a fitting retirement for the work they have done. However, with care the active life of a lurcher can be lengthened considerably. Premature entering, working a lurcher when it is patently obvious that the sapling is too young to work is a fairly certain way of shortening rather than lengthening the working life of a lurcher. A lurcher worked before its muscles and organs have had time to mature has in fact an extremely short working life.

Good diet, good kennel management all contribute to lengthening the working life of a lamping lurcher and commonsense rather than the strict rule of thumb should govern the way a lurcherman treats his lamping dog. Contrary to most tales, few lurchermen live in districts where rabbits are so numerous that a fit, strong dog can be run to death pursuing them. Most field fatalities among lurchers occur in the early days of the rabbiting season from September onwards when a bountiful supply of rabbits has to be worked by a dog that is sluggish and unfit because of the summer lay off. Running dogs need a good six weeks of hardening-off training – a time when exercise is increased and a diet with a higher protein level is fed to the in-training dog. A dog simply taken from kennels after a summer rest and run hard at lamped rabbits is irreparably damaged or injured by the night's venture.

After six weeks of walking, gentle exercise and light lamping to finally harden-off the lurcher, the dog is usually fit enough to ensure it is ready for a hard, testing lamping season. If a dog is in hard, fit condition and is not injury-prone then the lurcher can be run hard perhaps three nights a week. To work a dog more frequently than this is a sure-fire method of prematurely ageing a lurcher. A lurcher really needs lay-off days to ensure damaged muscle tissue is repaired and the lurcher has time to mentally recuperate. Dogs that are worked each and every night of the season often develop a sluggish, lacklustre attitude when lamping – an indication that the dog is far from in top form.

After each and every night's lamping the lurcher should be carefully examined for cuts, rips, tears in its fur and flesh and, more important, damage to its feet. Like a racehorse, a lurcher too is only as sound as its feet. Toes are seldom knocked up during a single night's lamping and warning signs that all is not well with the toes can be observed days before the actual injury manifests itself. Toes that are suspect will often be slightly swollen and sore to touch days before they are finally pushed out of alignment with the rest of the foot. I believe rest and professional treatment can prevent most of the damaged toes many lurchers display.

A lurcher should not be fed the day before it is required to lamp and should always be run sharp set though never in a famished condition. A famished animal will usually fade badly during the course of a hard night's lamping and will seldom give of its best. Lamping dogs should be eager to feed once they return home however, and appear ravenous when they perceive that food is about to be offered. A dog that is not ravenous after a long and testing hunt is an unwell dog, as is a dog that will sooner sleep than eat. A lurcher should wolf its food and show a desire to sleep only after it has fed well. A dog with no appetite, particularly if the dog appears drowsy and lacklustre after a hunt, should be suspect, and if the dog appears jaded and unwell the day following the hunt expert veterinary help should be sought. Lurchers are often quite severely damaged during a hunt – internally bruised with damaged hearts, lungs and diaphragms – yet may display no external signs of damage. The behaviour of a lurcher immediately after a lamping session tells the lamper much of the condition of the dog. Hence when the lamper returns home and puts his lamp on charge a few minutes spent watching the lurcher is time well spent. However, a dog that appears jaded or ill for days after a lamping session needs expert professional treatment, not homespun remedies and nostrums. Lampers who work their dogs very hard in country that is well stocked with rabbits frequently resort to the use of electrolyte solutions to revive jaded dogs. Twenty years ago most lampers would have disdained the use of these mineral/glucose mixtures but the modern lamper is a more scientific and sensible hunter.

It is extremely bad stockmanship for the lamper not to observe the behaviour of the lurcher when it returns from each and every run. A fit, healthy, sound lurcher will be ready and eager to run again once it has returned to hand with or without its catch. A dog that remains at heel, still panting from the exertions of the previous run is not ready to run again and only when the lurcher is breathing normally should it be run at another rabbit. I watch for signs of exhaustion in a lurcher and return home when I observe the dog is weary. I never continue hunting until the dog is reeling with exhaustion, though I have seen dogs run in pitiful states and still attempt to catch their rabbits. It is in fact a tragedy that some of the noblest and gamest of dogs are in the hands of the very worst dog trainers. Hancock records that he has sold as many as five lurchers to hunters in a ten year period and most of the dogs have been run until they were incapable of further performances in the field. Yet in the hands of competent trainers lurchers will give seven or eight years of active service in the field.

The British countryside is an enigma. It is some of the most beautiful countryside in the world, yet a lurcher running over such country is often in desperate danger. Pitfalls and deathtraps abound in the fields of Britain. Quarries, craters dug to extract building stone, are seldom completely filled and are often used for refuse tips for the most dangerous objects imaginable – antique farm equipment mingled with old deep freezers, refrigerators and cookers are often laced with tangles of rusted barbed wire. These craters often act as sanctuaries for rabbits, for the refuse affords good drainage that is essential in a breeding warren, but a dog pursuing a rabbit into such a tangle is in desperate danger. Hancock's diaries records that many of the dogs he has bred and sold have come to grief in these rubbish-filled craters.

Ancient farm machinery left in the corners of or around the edges of fields is equally dangerous to the lamping lurcher. A brush against rusted harrow tines can often disembowel a dog running at top speed. Indeed I once saw an excellent lurcher, a great catch dog and a fine retriever, come to grief in such a way. Its owner, a young woman who had competed with the animal in obedience tests and lurcher jumping events, was mortified at the damage done to her dog that died in seconds after the collision with the harrow and never again lamped or kept a lurcher.

A dog brushing against a barbed wire tine that is virtually invisible in darkness is also in great danger and, once again, I have seen dogs that have been terribly damaged by a brush with a barbed wire tine. In a Lichfield vet's waiting room I once saw a lurcher that had brushed against a barbed wire strand and had not only sustained a gash that stretched from neck to rump but such was the nature of the rip that a huge flap of skin had parted company with the muscle covering the rib cage and hung nearly to floor level. When the youth brought the dog into the waiting room grown men turned pale but such was the skill of one of the veterinary surgeons that the dog was stitched up and recovered from its terrible injury. Other dogs would have been less lucky however.

It is excellent policy for the lamper to know the country he is about to lamp and to avoid places where hazards can kill or injure his dog, no matter how many rabbits inhabit such areas. I always walk the country I am to lamp by daylight hours and look out for pitfalls and damages that are likely to be present. This may seem a little inconvenient for the would-be lamper, but such a practice will reduce the damage a dog might incur.

13

The Pursuit of Deer with Lurchers

When one considers that Britain is a rather small, heavily populated country, it is amazing that it boasts more species of wild deer than most other countries in the world. Yet only two species of deer, the red and the roe are truly native to Britain.

Despite the fact that the general public associates the red deer, the largest species of deer in Britain – the 'Monarch of the Glen' of Landseer – with the wild, barren glens of Scotland or the rolling moorland of Dartmoor, the red deer is a woodland species. During Anglo-Norman times the species lived in the forests of England and Scotland and grew to a size which is greater than the largest Scottish deer taken today. A fifteen-stone stag would be considered a trophy specimen today, yet during Norman and Angevin times red deer grew to a much larger size, possibly because the forest deer were better nourished or possibly because trophy hunting has succeeded in reducing the average size of the species. Whatever the reason, it is likely the deer pursued by the Cathar, King William Rufus, were considerably larger than the largest trophy stags bagged in the Highlands today.

It takes a particularly strong and powerful lurcher to pull down a red deer stag single-handed. In fact, even before the Napoleonic War when the deerhound had brought about the extinction of the wolf in Scotland and northern England there were few single hounds that were capable of pulling down a red stag. In fact a strong red stag was often considered more than a match for a matched pair of deerhounds – though it should be pointed out that the deerhound Buscar, described by M'Neill in 1886, was a mere 28 inches at the shoulder and weighed 85 pounds – a considerably smaller animal than the deerhound of today, smaller, in fact, than the deerhound/greyhound long dogs that are favoured by deer poachers of today.

However, the red stag is a mighty fighter and there are many tales of stags that have taken a stand against a rockface and slain two or more deerhounds with their antlers. Modern deer poachers are wont to slip four or five hounds, usually deerhound/greyhound long dogs, at a stag and the result of the conflict is bloody, unsporting and damnably cruel. Deer so attacked are usually hideously lacerated and not infrequently disembowelled by the onslaughts of these dogs. Deerhound blood usually gives the long dog the necessary stature to bring down a red deer – indeed deerhound long dogs are still referred to as staghounds by itinerants.

Few sporting bodies support or favour the pursuit of deer with long dogs or lurchers. Indeed in Scotland where this deerhound hybrid finds a ready market the pursuit and capture of deer with dogs of any sort is illegal. Yet lampers using deerhound hybrids are a serious problem when deer are of economic importance. Basically, red deer fall into three categories in the Highlands:

> Farmed deer – deer bred for venison and fed hay and concentrates when provender is scarce;
> deer that live wild but are fed hay in hard winters;
> deer that are fed no supplementary feed.

Most of the deer killed by poachers' lurchers are in fact tame farmed deer that have little chance of escaping and the stags are so used to dogs that they put up little fight against the attacking lurchers.

Roe are truly wild deer, living solitary lives, dwelling in small groups, feeding on cultivated land during the hours of darkness and lying up in woodland or deep unburnt heather during the daylight hours. Roe are considerably smaller than red deer – though seventy-pound bucks have been killed from time to time – and most lurchers are more than capable of catching roe deer. There are in fact many instances of whippets pulling and holding mature roe deer. Indeed, the introduction of the Standfast Press epic *Coursing* – now a collector's piece – contains an account of a show-bred whippet catching and holding a roe deer by the throat. At the time of writing it should be added that roe venison sells for roughly three times the price paid for red deer venison but roe are so sparsely distributed that poachers rarely chance on them and hence find it easier meat – a bad but intentional pun – to set packs of large, powerful lurchers on park-bred red deer.

Fallow deer, the deer of parks and stately homes, often fall victim to poachers' lurchers. Many lurchers that will chase, catch and kill roe deer are more reluctant to pursue and catch fallow deer. Roe are solitary animals but fallow usually live in small herds and the thunder of hooves is often disconcerting to many lurchers. Fallow are amongst the fastest deer, vying with the brown hare for the title of 'Fastest British Mammalian Athlete'.

Yet the fallow deer is savagely poached and more fallow deer fall victim to the onslaught of poachers than any other species of deer. This fact is easily explained. Fallow are often park deer and are prevented from roaming by deer-proof fences that surround these parks. Hence, poachers use their dogs to cut out single deer, run the deer against the fence and hold the deer until the poacher (thief is a more accurate word from a legalistic point of view) arrives to cut the deer's throat and gut the deer. The famous Attingham Park slaughter encouraged magistrates to come down heavily on deer poachers, yet the poaching of deer on nearby Cannock Chase continued despite the massive publicity the Attingham Park issue gave the deer poacher. Convicted deer poachers are usually given sentences quite out of proportion to the damage they have done to deer. Two of the Attingham Park poachers pleaded 'Not guilty' and received eighteen months in prison. The third pleaded 'Guilty' but was already serving a suspended sentence and he too received eighteen months in prison. A week later a youth who robbed an elderly lady received six months in prison for his crimes.

Unlike the red and the roe the fallow is not a native of Great Britain. Though who introduced the deer into Britain and when they were brought to these islands has long been debated by naturalists and historians alike. G. J Millais believes the Phoenicians introduced the deer to Britain but offers no proof of his theory other than the fact that fallow deer were natives of southern Europe and the Phoenicians were great travellers. However by Roman times the fallow deer was established in Britain and by the seventeenth century many English counties boasted a greater head of fallow deer than the whole of continental Europe. These deer were kept in enclosed parks and it was only during the Civil War that escapees really established them in the wild. South-eastern England now boasts an incredible head of these dappled deer, though the species boasts a wide variety of colour variations ranging from nearly black to white.

Like the fallow deer the now common sika deer is not a native of Britain but unlike the fallow it has not only adapted well to the harsh conditions of the north of Britain but succeeded in hybridising with the native red deer. Unlike the fallow, the sika are pugnacious and very aggressive and potentially dangerous – there are numerous instances of these deer standing their ground when they are approached by a man – yet stags, even during the mating season, are extremely dog-shy; a small vocal terrier belonging to a picnicking party is reputed to have put to flight a stag that was about to attack a keeper. The deer has been known in Britain since 1860 when a pair were presented to the Zoological Society and housed at Regent Park. However, later that year a German animal dealer Johan Christian Karl Jamrach brought in a stag and three hind and allowed the quartet to breed on his estate in Enniskerry, County Wicklow and it is from this quartet all British sika deer have descended. The sika is smaller than the British red deer, the stags weighing in at about 120 pounds and the hinds seldom topping 85 pounds. The venison of the sika closely resembles the meat of the red deer and fetches roughly the same price – considerably less than the venison of the roe, one should add.

Chinese water deer often give the impression of running like rather large, clumsy hares. The majority of these deer are roughly 25 to 30 pounds in weight and hence can seldom over-match even a whippet-sized lurcher. Their teeth and tusks can be used to good effect if harassed or attacked by dogs but the species seems unlikely to be commonly encountered in Britain. Fawns weighing less than a pound are extremely vulnerable to predators and there is a tale of a water deer being reared by a Shropshire farmer's wife after the housecat had brought home the newly-born fawn.

Muntjac, both the Chinese, or Reeve's, muntjac and the Indian muntjac are confined to the south-east of Britain and are roughly the same size, some 25 pounds in weight, though the Indian species is slightly larger. Hybrids between the two forms are not uncommon and both species live as solitaries or in pairs. When pursued by dogs, and most lurchers are enthusiastic about chasing them, muntjac run as though injured, head held high and rump elevated. So such as to the species of deer found in Britain and now the laws protecting these species.

The law is so severe that the wise lurcherman avoids hunting deer of any sort. A thousand years of legislation governs the hunting of cervids and courts are well-geared to deal with deer poachers. Few lurcher owners have permission to hunt deer of any sort, in fact.

In Scotland it is forbidden to hunt deer of any sort with dogs, in England and Wales it is an offence to hunt deer by night and, as landowners will rarely give lurchermen the permission needed to hunt deer on the land, most deer taken by lurchers are poached. It is also an offence to kill any red, roe, fallow or sika deer during the closed season (muntjac and water deer breed the year round, so it appears). The Deer Act of 1963 Section I defines the closed season as, 'Red – male – 1st of May to 31st of July; female – 1st of March to 31st of October'. Fallow and sika enjoy the same closed season but the roe should not be disturbed from the 1st of March to 31st of October though the males are protected from the 1st of November to 31st of March; it must be added that both wild and farmed deer enjoy the same closed season. Thus the species of deer found in Britain and the laws protecting those deer and the penalty for poaching or stealing deer are severe by any standards. These penalties should always be borne in mind when the lurcherman ventures into country where deer are likely to be encountered and the said lurcherman would do well to give any species of deer a miss.

14

The Pursuit of Fox with Lurchers and Long Dogs

The rather neat epigram, 'It is not the size of the dog in the fight but the size of the fight in the dog', comes to mind as I write this chapter, for I have witnessed a nineteen-inch lurcher of indeterminate breeding run, bowl and kill three foxes that were beaten and driven from bracken a dozen miles from my home. A giant, elegant long dog bred, perhaps, not in the purple but with bulk and strength enough to pull down a musk ox watched the spectacle of the spikey-coated whippet-sized dog at work with interest but refrained from joining in. It is in fact true that the disposition of the dog more than the size of the lurcher is more important in a lurcher destined to take fox, but with careful entering it is possible to enter most sighthounds to fox catching.

Some dogs, obviously, show a natural disposition to catch fox; it is, in fact, quite rare to find a retired coursing greyhound that has coursed and caught hares during its working life that will not eagerly course and catch fox. Hancock of Sutton Coldfield is of the opinion that some dogs show an almost instinctive propensity to tackle foxes though even these dogs need to be entered properly to make them more efficient fox catchers. Hancock states that he asks clients if they wish the puppy he is selling to be used for fox catchers and then advises the would-be fox catcher to purchase a puppy sired by a particular stud dog that has a good record for producing fox catchers. Likewise, Hancock has remarked that some of his stud dogs seldom produce lurchers that show a great deal of interest to course and catch foxes. It should also be noted that my own strain of lurcher seldom produce dogs that willingly enter to fox, though they are seldom given an opportunity to test their mettle on large quarry, one must add. However, when I did keep dogs primarily to course and catch foxes I went through a fairly elaborate process of entering the puppy to fox and found that my careful entering programme usually paid dividends, though, once again, I must confess I had some fairly heretical views about entering lurchers to foxes and I believe that much depends on the lurcher's first contact with fox and the mood of the dog when he first encounters his first fox.

Basically, there are three methods of catching foxes with lurchers – a) lamping foxes – foxes are nocturnal and are seldom seen during the daylight hours; b) coursing foxes that have been bolted by terriers; or c) slipping lurchers on foxes that have been driven from cover by sundry types of dog and beaters.

The process of entering a lurcher to fox is roughly the same whether the foxes are to be lamped or taken during the daylight hours and while it is true that no lurcher, long dog or sighthound should be allowed to course or tackle a fox until it has experience of coursing smaller quarry, preliminary training before entering makes it easier for the lurcherman to enter his ward to fox.

I confess I often cause consternation by stopping my car or van to pick up road casualty cadavers that litter country roads. Rabbits and hares are fed to my dogs while the great variety of gulls that have been knocked down while feeding on other road casualties – the biter bit perhaps – are used to feed my ferrets. Foxes are always picked up – that is if they are not too damaged by passing vehicles – and I make excellent use of the fox cadavers to enter both lurchers and terriers. I encourage both types of dog to worry the carcases of fox, even attaching lines to the hind legs of the cadavers, dragging the carcase in front of lurchers and encouraging the dogs to chase and seize the dead fox. If the lurcher can be encouraged to shake the cadaver so much the better and some lurchers develop such a passion for shaking the carcase of a fox that they will exhaust themselves in the process. Aherne's Grip, a deerhound/greyhound hybrid, in its youth a great fox catcher, would shake the carcase of a fox until the dog became so exhausted it would topple with the exhaustion induced by its hatred of the dead fox. It is likely that Grip was a somewhat disturbed animal but many lurchers will attack fox cadavers with the same enthusiasm. Hancock noted that any fox left within the reach of his three-quarter bred collie/greyhound Romulus was given the occasional shake by the dog as it passed near the cadaver.

Cadavers can be used to encourage a lurcher to seize and rag until the carcase becomes too decayed to use. Many fox hunters simply hang fox carcases out of reach of young lurchers and the movements of the wind-blown cadaver will often encourage the lurcher to jump and pull at the corpse. This type of pre-entering training cannot be overdone – unless, that is, the lurcher shows signs of sickening of the game of ragging dead foxes. When I lived near the A38 I had access to an incredible number of dead foxes, road casualties for the most part, and had little or no difficulty starting my lurchers to foxes during this time. It should be added that I still keep the self-same strain of lurcher, but because of the absence of fox cadavers on the most northerly part of the A9 my lurchers show little interest in coursing and catching foxes that sometimes appear during the rabbiting season.

I would never consider entering a lurcher to fox until the dog had become dextrous at catching rabbits or hares. Foxes are agile and nimble rather than fast animals, but they often outrun quite athletic lurchers – though many of these lurchers are obviously not trying as hard as they would at rabbits or hares. However, once a dog becomes an efficient catch dog and has shown a degree of maturity it can be considered as ready to course and catch foxes.

The first encounter a dog has with the running fox is all-important and may determine how the dog will react to fox for the rest of its life. I like to enter a dog that is wildly excited by the prospect of a chase and a catch rather than a dog that is phlegmatic and emotionless when it sees its first fox. Some phlegmatic dogs are often extraordinarily good fox killers, however. Some years ago an Essex-based hunter known as Paul Fowles bought one of the first of David Hancock's Taffy puppies. It will be of interest to historians studying the development of the modern lurcher (Taffy must be the most prolific lurcher stud dog in history) to know that Hancock viewed Taffy's first puppies with some reservation, for they matured quickly but had a stoical attitude to life and were decidedly chary of strangers. Fowles dog seldom showed any excitement even when its owner came to take him out and showed little excitement when a rabbit, hare or fox appeared in the beam. When slipped at fox, however, he struck them forcibly and the fox was dead seconds after the dog made contact with it. It should be of interest to collectors of lurcher tales that Fowles' dog mated a variety of bitches but seldom produced outstanding progeny.

Frankly, I like to see a dog that is frantically excited before it is slipped on a fox, and if this means delaying the slipping of the dog until the lurcher is suitably excited I delay the process until the dog is fired up. Many dogs will course a fox with enthusiasm but refrain from attempting to catch the animal. An excited dog heated up by the prospect of the chase will usually attempt to seize its fox and becomes infuriated rather than deterred when the fox retaliates. When a lurcher or long dog runs a fox half-heartedly – and it may surprise the tyro lurcherman to realise just how many lurchers will deliberately run half-heartedly to avoid making contact with a fox – the dog is often deterred by the first bite from its adversary. Hence, firing up a dog by whatever means the handler thinks fitting is permissible before the lurcher/long dog is slipped. Dogs that are not heated by the prospect of a battle with a fox will make incongruous, unrealistic feints at the quarry, attempt to shoulder-charge the animal or even make an almost indifferent attempt to seize the rump of the fox. They will seldom course the quarry with the fury that is required to catch the fox.

When young, inexperienced dogs show such an attitude a new interest in fox coursing can sometimes be rekindled if the puppy is run in conjunction with an experienced fox coursing/fox catching dog. This will sometimes generate interest in seizing the fox rather than running alongside it. The older, more experienced dog gives the youngster a sense of competition and this may well generate the enthusiasm that is necessary for a lurcher to become an efficient fox catcher. If a dog shows no enthusiasm for the fight when it observes another dog take the fight to the fox, a few more sessions of running the dog in a couple may generate the necessary interest in the activity.

Some dogs will never generate the necessary degree of enthusiasm for fox coursing no matter how many times they are run in couples. Perhaps the failure of these dogs is due to some innate disposition that determines the dog will never display antipathy to foxes. It is more likely, however, that the lurcher has not been trained and heated up before its first encounter with fox.

Once the lurcher is wed to fox and will engage the fox from any angle during the course – many dogs will not face the fox head-on and dally to obtain a rump or long hold, the entering of the fox catching lurcher is virtually complete and lurchers and long dogs seldom forget fox catching skills. Yet the fox catching dog needs a great deal of practice to perfect the skills it has to acquire and, make no bones about it, foxes are particularly tricky animals for a dog to course. In open country, over lawn-like fields most lurchers find little difficulty coming to terms with a fox. Yet in the middle of an open field a fox will somehow find a rabbit burrow into which it can dive to escape the strike of a lurcher, or even an undulation in the field to throw off its pursuer.

More years ago than I care to remember I owned a very game, tough, old bitch called Penguin. One day while ferreting the Dyatt Estate in Lichfield a particularly tenacious hob ferret pushed out a small, weedy vixen that struck out into the middle of a huge ploughed field, a field both Penguin and I knew well. Penguin had many faults but she ran foxes fearlessly. The vixen scarcely larger than a twelve-week old cub was obviously in desperate danger as Penguin closed with it in seconds, bowling the tiny vixen twice, yet, miraculously, the fox found a tiny crack in the rocks exposed by the plough – a hole into which a rabbit would have trouble squeezing – and thus escaped capture. I saw her frequently for about two years after she had appeared on the estate and each time she evaded my dogs, gliding into woods, copses, running along the muddy bed of the brood escaping death by a dozen different ploys. There are no happy endings in nature, no happy ever after finales to the lives of any wild mammals. One morning on the way to work I found her emaciated body on the roadside near the estate. She weighed less than six pounds and was razor-thin. What illness had caused the decline of this creature is unknown, she was in pitiful condition, yet she had managed to evade numerous lampers for several years.

Foxes are largely nocturnal feeders, so lampers frequently encounter them on hunting forays. If a lamper with lurcher in the act of returning a squealing rabbit to hand turns and flashes the beam around the field behind him, the chances are the lamp will illuminate a pair of huge saucer-like eyes of a fox whose curiosity has drawn it to watch the spectacle of a dog chasing rabbits illuminated by a beam of light. However, to persuade these foxes to come close enough to afford the lurcher a sporting chance of catching them is a different matter. A fox will watch a lamping party with interest – but only from a safe distance.

There are various ways of ensuring that a fox comes close enough to the lamper and his lurcher so that the lurcher has at least a chance to catch its quarry. Many lampers swear by squeaking in the fox. Squeaking in involves the lamper pursing his lips and uttering a squeaking sound that is said to resemble a distressed or hurt rabbit. Few lampers are capable mimics and those who are are seldom more efficient at calling in foxes than some of the very worst distressed rabbit impersonators. I do not believe that even the most dewy-eyed cub is fooled by the lamper squeaking in the middle of a field. Foxes are curious creatures but certainly not stupid beasts, and I doubt if any fox believes that the squeaking sound is being emitted by a rabbit. Foxes will investigate any sound that is neither too loud nor clearly made by an organism that is hostile to foxes. I have many times squeaked in foxes to a distance of ten or so feet. Likewise, I have brought foxes equally close by clicking two stones together.

It is when foxes approach the lamper that the importance of the basic obedience training he has taught to his lurcher begins to show. The lurcher should remain stock-still either at the sit position or fastened by a leash as the fox approaches the lamper and the dog should neither pull towards the fox nor whine in anticipation of the course that may follow. A vocal dog, even a dog that whines and sobs slightly, will alert any fox to the dangers it is about to encounter and once the fox is startled it will usually turn its head away from the beam, lose its eyes in the darkness and literally vanish from sight with a speed that will amaze both the lamper and his lurcher.

Once the fox has been lured in close enough to afford the lurcher a fair chance of capturing the animal the lurcher should be slipped or encouraged to course the fox. It would be ludicrous to suggest just how close a fox should approach the lamping party before the lamper slips his dogs.

In wooded country a short slip is required, for a fox will almost certainly head for cover once it becomes aware of the presence of danger. In flat or open country the lurcher will often be able to catch its fox even if the quarry is given quite a lot of law, but the lamper should always realise that a fox will use every irregular feature of the landscape to escape capture – and it is wise to allow too short a slip rather than to allow the animal fair law when one is lamping foxes.

Another method of luring foxes close enough for the lamper to slip a lurcher at them is known as 'salting'. Salting consists of placing offal or some aromatic type of meat in the middle of an open field to attract foxes to feed in situations where they can be lamped and coursed with lurchers. Foxes find the most incredibly pungent waste attractive. In 1987 I salted down haddock waste to bait lobster creels, but the salt failed to preserve the fish and the haddock degenerated into a slimy paste that stank of ammonia. I bagged the waste to tip into the sea, but the foxes came for miles to eat the filthy waste, chewing their way through the plastic bag to eat the eye-watering rotting fish. It should be added that rabbits were numerous in the fields around my croft. In Lichfield I used rancid turkey offal to good effect – though the Lichfield area which lies due south of the Meynell Hunt country and due west of the Atherstone country hosts an incredible number of foxes.

When I regularly sought out foxes to lamp I would place offal in the centre of fields for a week or so before I decided to hunt them. In one field near Whittington Hurst I salted the land from the time the corn was cut though I seldom began lamping foxes until late in November when the pelts had ceased to moult. By this time foxes were coming for miles to feed and I caught thirty foxes within a circle of a mile or so radius in November-December 1982.

By far the best lure to bring foxes into a field is the presence of a cadaver of another fox. At one time I lamped foxes for Cyril Bicknell, David Hancock's brother-in-law, to shoot. If we left down the carcase of a fox Cyril shot for more than a few minutes another fox would come to investigate the corpse. One night I simply left the corpse of one fox in the middle of a field near Cottage Farm and an incredible number of foxes came and sniffed the cadaver and some attempted to haul the carcase away. I have never connected this action with that of an elephant herd attempting to haul away a wounded member of that herd. Foxes find most carrion attractive and once the cadaver had cooled other foxes simply regarded the corpse as edible carrion.

Hence the policy of leaving a fox carcase in a field until the night's lamping is over, rather than carrying the fox around the field, is a policy any lamper should adopt. It is certainly the most productive method of luring foxes to an area – and the reader would be astounded to realise just how many foxes exist in Britain. Most Midland towns are fairly well-infested with foxes and, so it seems, with rabbits. In January 1990 Lal Hardy showed me around the back roads of Muswell Hill, London – a populous district through which I would be reluctant to attempt to drive a car. The gardens, wasteland and tiny parks were populated by numerous rabbits and a surprising number of foxes. Likewise when I travelled to work along Spaghetti Junction, the world's most popular racetrack perhaps, the motorway was often littered with road casualty animals including foxes and, more amazingly, badgers which were also finding rich pickings in the centres of cities. There is, in fact, some evidence to suggest that cities are far from the sterile, concrete jungles many ecologists believe them to be and may well be havens for wildlife. The attitude of city dwellers is somewhat different from that of the countryman. Foxes are seen as curiosities by the city dweller and are coaxed, fed and sheltered by the urban based population. Countrymen are conditioned, from birth perhaps, to regard the fox as a pest that must be killed on sight. Small wonder more and more foxes are moving into the cities. Furthermore it should be mentioned that while it is perfectly legal to lamp and kill (as humanely as possible) any fox a lurcherman encounters during a night's lamping in the country, there are somewhat antique Acts of Parliament that forbid the lurcherman causing or allowing his dog to kill a fox in urban surroundings. The time may well come when foxes become so numerous as to be a nuisance in towns and cities, but the enormous number of road casualty foxes found in any Midland town must surely act as a powerful control measure to ensure that city foxes never become very numerous.

I have never favoured the hunting of two or more lurchers together and dislike terrier/lurcher combinations intensely. These combinations which, in theory, involve the terrier working deep cover and pushing the rabbit out so the lurcher can course the animal usually result in bedlam, with the terrier chasing the rabbit-carrying lurcher around the field and the lurcher refusing to come to hand with its catch. Brawls involving terriers and lurchers, the outcome of which are predetermined by the size of the lurcher, are all too common and very unpleasant, to say the least.

I never allow terriers to accompany my lurchers and avoid the company of those who enjoy such chaos, and reader, chaos accurately describes the sheer bedlam that always accompanies working a lurcher in conjunction with any breed of dog.

However, I have seen efficient terrier/lurcher combinations used to bolt, catch and kill foxes; but even these combinations are all too prone to riot situations accompanying them. In theory the lurcher should stand above the earth while the terrier works fox in the bowels of the said earth. When the fox has been persuaded to bolt, a lurcher courses the fox and pulls it down, killing it quickly or holding the animal until the handler arrives to despatch the fox equally quickly. In theory this works well and, indeed, I have caught many foxes this way, but likewise I have seen many of these hunts result in unpleasant brawls. One such encounter is worth relating.

Sometime in 1981 I bought the elderly Jack Russell terrier Pip from Errol Forsyth to bring in new blood to what was becoming a very inbred snipey-headed strain of terrier that I kept primarily to hunt rat. Pip was a veteran when I bought him – a ten-year old legend in his own lifetime that had not only sired half the winning terriers in Durham and Northumberland but was as true a worker to fox as a man could ask. He was related to my own terriers but not so closely as to bring about problems when he was introduced into the strain, but his reputation as a worker was such that I could not resist trying the dog one last time, so to speak.

At the same time as I owned Pip David Hancock owned two lurchers, Timmy and Romulus, and while Timmy was a shade shy of head-on encounters with foxes – one could scarcely blame him – Romulus had an implacable hatred of all things vulpine and would race into the open jaws of any fox rather than allow the creature to escape. In fact, despite his gentle disposition – David's daughter often dressed him in ski suits or dresses – I have yet to see a more determined fox catching lurcher.

So, the characters set; the all too obvious scenario followed. That year Dyatt Woods, Whittington, housed an incredible number of foxes, so great almost in fact that it became difficult to raise pheasants for the shoot that flourished on the estate. Hence we tried Pip one last time before retiring him to stud. Pip marked an inhabited earth – a long vacated badger sett as it happened – and David held both dogs on slips near the earth while Pip entered and began to give tongue. (If I might digress a little, I have never favoured David's methods of holding a lurcher on the slip while a terrier works a fox, but his methods are his own as he describes in his books.)Pip stayed nearly an hour before the fox decided to bolt and Pip was hot on its heels as it left the earth.

Romulus and Timmy turned the fox off its route and Pip seized and held the animal until Romulus killed the fox with a single bite and a shake. However, Romulus had an implacable hatred of foxes and continued to shake the cadaver, and Pip, until we arrived to stop the combat. Pip was badly winded and bruised by the encounter and ever afterwards had a deep suspicion of any lurcher. If David had allowed the dogs liberty to wander and secure the fox above the earth I believe the situation would never have germinated, let alone borne fruit, but different people develop different techniques and Hancock believes my own training methods should also be questioned. I never restrict a lurcher that is working a fox in conjunction with a terrier. I believe that allowing the dog to wander atop the earth fulfils two functions. Firstly, it encourages a bond between the lurcher and the terrier – they are working in conjunction with one another – although either will jealously guard the prey from the other. Secondly, a fox may bolt from any number of earth entrances/exits and a lurcher is able to follow the progress of the battle below ground and to be stationed near the hole from which the fox will bolt. Curiously such a lurcher may well outpace a fox – foxes are not particularly swift animals though they are amazingly agile – a lurcher has but to lose sight of a fox to allow the creature every chance to escape. I have known many dogs – indeed I have owned many dogs – that would lose a fox, hunt it up by scent and then catch the fox, but I have known a great any more that have little olfactory sense and once a fox disappears from view are incapable of finding it. I've never liked lurchers that have a strong trace of sighthound in their ancestry as I believe that too much sighthound blood is scarcely conducive to producing a lurcher with a good nose. Foxes are far from easy catches even when they bolt under the very nose of a lurcher. Many times I saw Penguin, a bitch with an incredible nose, lose foxes in cover and return empty-jawed, so to speak. A fox on the run will use every obstacle to its advantage and succeed in disappearing into the most tiny hole imaginable. I have always kept finely-built terriers that would not only rat at great speed but could find their ways into very narrow crevices, yet I have seen many fox run to ground in earths and burrows into which a rabbit would have trouble in squeezing. A fox knows every earth, sett, burrow or crevice in the locality of its lair and will certainly use all its wiles to escape capture. Not for nothing is the fox the sly, evasive, cunning creature of European folk legend, for the species has an ability to escape capture even when capture seems a certainty. 'Reynard's Last Run' Masefield's truly great, rolling, flowing epic shows only a fraction of the wiles a hard-pressed fox would show. When Reynard found the earth blocked, 'barred with stakes', the chances are he would have found another warren, sett or earth nearby and escaped into the hole inches ahead of the hounds.

I dislike protracted dog/fox battles – so beloved by those who will surely bring an end to fieldsports by their activities – and hence I consider it a duty to kill foxes as quickly and humanely as possible with as little unpleasantness as is possible when the death of an animal is concerned. A sharp blow from a heavy stick will normally kill a fox quickly and cleanly. Protracted battles are messy, nasty and often cause considerable damage to the dog. Even small bites, tiny nicks that go unnoticed amongst the facial furnishing of the most hirsute lurchers are prone to fester and cause great pain to the lurcher. The shorter the battle between the dog and the fox the more easily the lurcher recovers to hunt another day.

Small whippet-sized lurchers will catch and sometimes kill foxes. Walsh and Lowe, authors of *The English Whippet*, show just such a whippet badly torn after an encounter with a fox, but it is bad policy to expect a very small lurcher or long dog to kill its fox unaided. Some dogs develop an incredible technique of disposing of foxes quickly and, seemingly, with little effort. A famous fox catching dog in his day was Terry Aherne's Grip, an Ardkinglas deerhound/greyhound hybrid, a tall, mean dog, docile with children perhaps, but a deadly foe in battle. In the days prior to the 1981 Wildlife and Countryside Act, and even before the 1973 Badger Protection Act, Grip regularly caught lamped badgers which he released on command and returned to hand. Foxes were shoulder-charged with such force that Grip had little need to shake them after the collision and he passed on his strange technique to some of his puppies; Michael Hoyle's dog, a dog that won at Lambourn, caught foxes using the self same technique and so did others of Grip's progeny. One of his puppies, bred out of Ann Power's Lambourn winning strain, was the softest-mouthed bitch imaginable and would carry chicks to hand, dampened by spittle perhaps, but otherwise unharmed. As a fox courser she was incredibly efficient. At Melton Mowbray where I saw her run in 1984 she passed over her fox seemingly without touching it and returned to hand without shaking the fox. I ran to the scene of what I considered to be a missed catch only to find a fox with a dislocated neck lying in a hollow in the field. Grip gave rise to a remarkable line of lurcher, athletic, furious fox catchers, though brainless and virtually untrainable for any of the more complex skills required of a lurcher. Some of his puppies were exported to the USA and absorbed into the cold-blood greyhound lines (long dogs rather than lurchers) and coursed and hunted wolves. Grip was of a line I used on my own bitches but found the progeny difficult to train and rather stupid. Terry Aherne kept nothing back from this dog for he too disliked the recalcitrant nature of Grip's progeny, but there are still many lurchers bred from this dog in and around Staffordshire.

Grip's long dog/lurcher line fell out of favour in the late 1980s when, because the line was no longer maintained carefully and possibly because the dogs bred from Grip were seldom versatile enough to be classed as all-round lurchers, Hancock's Eynock stock superseded these deerhound/greyhounds with the fox catching fraternity. This line is now very fashionable and also very typey and deserves mention. Hancock's stud Richard Jones had mated an Eland/Minnesota bitch greyhound and bred Taffy and Wendell, two half-bred lurchers. In the first litter the unfortunate Linnet was born but was crippled during her first season and limped for ever after, later damage to her tail (due to an irritating kennel habit known as tail whip) caused her tail to be amputated and hence she appeared to be a rather hideous looking dog. The line, however, was tractable – indeed, the NLRC Scottish trials representative owned by Jim Bell was of this breeding – but had a reputation for being dour and surly. Later Hancock mated Linnet to her sire Richard Jones (a border/bearded collie hybrid) and bred what are now referred to as reverse three-quarter breds – collie/greyhound to collie – dogs which are seldom fast enough to catch hares but versatile enough to be retrievers, long netting dogs and lamping dogs. Chris Wain of Adlington used one of these hybrids for a variety of purposes. However, a litter brother of Wain's bitch was Hancock's Eynock (named after a Midland cartoon character). Eynock was to become the sire of some of the most famous fox catching dogs in lurcher history. Hancock mated him to a series of top flight coursing greyhounds and hence bred the now famous three/eighths/five/eighths hybrids – three/eighths collie, five/eigths greyhound – roughcoated, thick-skinned dogs which are used primarily as fox catching lurchers. These hybrids are now favoured by many pelt hunters, though recently there seems to have been a rebirth of interest in the popular deerhound/greyhound hybrids of the type bred by Nuttall in the late 1960s.

Prior to 1990 an amazing number of pit bull terrier/greyhounds were advertised in 'Shooting News'. However, the spate of American pit bull terrier attacks in 1991 provoked the editor of the magazine to exercise great caution in the choice of hybrids advertised in *Shooting News*. These pit bull terrier/greyhound hybrids were famed for their stamina as well as their aggression, though Peachey, writing as A. G. Fox in the same magazine, states that the production and sale of the pit bull hybrids is illegal under the provision of the Dangerous Dogs Act 1991. The reasons for the production of this hybrid are a little hazy – greyhounds pure and simple are certainly game enough to tackle any British quarry without further infusions of fighting dog blood. In fact, there seems to be little to gain from producing these hybrids and a lot to lose if the recommendations of the Dangerous Dogs Act 1991 are ever implemented.

15

Long Netting and Lurchers

Now, if ever there was a much debated subject the use of lurchers to drive to long nets is certainly one. Spaniels, retrievers and even collies are ideally suited to working with long nets – they have a strong inclination to hunt up quarry but little desire to seize and kill game that is entrapped and entangled in nets. Likewise the most unsuitable type of dog to work a long net would be a dog that showed a strong propensity not only to hunt up game but to pursue and to kill game, no matter where the quarry seeks to go. Terriers, greyhounds, long dogs and lurchers fall all too easily into this category and hence are the very devil to train to drive game to long nets – without, that is, following the said game into the net and creating the most unholy tangle imaginable.

A fast dog, a dog capable of running down rabbits and hares, is not required by the long netter. A slower dog, a steady dog that is easily controlled by the long netter is more desirable – though, frankly, just as a lurcher can easily be trained not to mouth rabbits in a purse net, lurchers can be taught not to attack game tangled in the long net – but once again, the long netter should exercise considerable care choosing the right type of lurcher to teach to drive to the long net.

Somewhere at some time there must have been pure bred sighthounds or true long dog composites that have been trained to a high enough standard to be able to shepherd game to a long net and not follow game into the net making the devil's own tangle, but I have yet to see one. Dennis Abbot tells tales of whippets that had been taught the skills required during the 1940s and 1950s, but seems uncertain whether these dogs were pure bred whippets or whippet/lurcher hybrids – collie, bull terrier or Bedlington terrier hybrids. Certainly whippets are a shade too quick-silver to be ideal long netter's dogs though, once again, certain people have patience and ability enough to teach complex tasks to the most amazing types of dogs.

For personal preference, a collie-bred or retriever-bred lurcher would be the only type of lurcher hybrid I would consider teaching to work in conjunction with a long net, though I have trained pure-bred GSDs to drive game to a long net, so no doubt a GSD/greyhound hybrid could also be taught to drive game. However, the ideal long netter's lurcher – and it has yet to be determined whether any type of lurcher makes an ideal long netter's dog – needs a strong baseline in order to be taught the restraint the long netter's dog needs to learn.

Just what are the skills a long netter's dog – be that dog a nonsighthound or a lurcher – should learn? Firstly, such a dog would need to learn how to sit and stay while a long net is being set up. Secondly, such a dog needs to be taught to drop to the lie or stay position instantly on command. Thirdly, such a dog needs to be taught to go away from the handler on command and to work back to the handler who, stationed behind the long net, despatches game that becomes entangled in the meshes of the net. Lastly, the dog would need to be taught that it must regard game that is entangled in the meshes of the net as verboten – an untrained dog will play the very devil with tangled game and cause terrific damage to both nets and quarry.

No lurcher that has not undergone an intensive obedience training programme should be taken out with the long net and the dog simply won't pick up the training in the field, so to speak. Once a dog is acquainted with catching quarry, rabbits, hares etc., it becomes difficult, though not impossible, to teach it to drive game to nets and yet leave both the game and the nets untouched.

The subject of teaching a dog to sit and to stay has been dealt with earlier at the start of the book, so it is expedient to assume the reader has acquired the techniques of teaching the dog these tasks. However, sending the dog away on command often confounds the beginner. Yet this is one of the most easily taught skills involved in teaching a dog to drive to a long net.

There are basically two methods of teaching a dog to go away, go to it or go with it – the command I use when training – and either method will teach a dog to raze a field to put the rabbits or what-have-you back to the nets, and while the exercise is often tedious and sometimes incredibly bewildering to the puppy, the exercise must be learned if the dog is to be of use to the long netter. Puppies often find being sent away, after they have been encouraged to come to hand, a shade confusing, but I repeat, the exercise must be learned if the dog is to drive game to a long net.

Professional handlers station a long, round, smooth pole firmly in the earth in the training field but a spade driven into a garden soil will suffice to train a puppy to go away from the handler. So with puppy on the leash the handler should approach the pole. When the handler is nearly level with the pole he should utter the words, 'Go on', or the equivalent, and send the puppy around the pole and back to the handler. It is a simple but confusing exercise for the puppy but one that should be rewarded with profuse praise. Each training session should involve increasing the distance between the handler, dog and pole, encouraging the puppy to move forward and walk around the pole. Eventually the leash is not long enough to allow the dog to walk forward, round the pole and return to the handler and I usually replace the leash with a length of coir line and encourage the whelp to run the entire length of line to round the pole.

Another method favoured by many obedience training club instructors is to sit the dog and for the handler to take an extended leash, walk around the pole and back to a position behind the sitting dog. The lead is tugged slightly and the words, 'Go forward' or 'Move on' uttered as the lead is pulled and the dog moves away from the handler. Tangles are almost inevitable, I'm afraid, and the handler should compensate for this upset caused when the dog twists the leash as it rounds the post by giving the lurcher profuse praise and petting the dog.

Eventually the use of the post can be disregarded and the dog sent away first on the leash and then running free. Puppies are invariably confused or bewildered by the go away or send away training so it is well to end each training session with a wild game to allow the puppy to forget the discomfort it has experienced during the send away training session.

John Holmes remarks that he trained his greyhound – a sighthound he trained to a truly remarkable level of obedience – to go away by a totally unique method once other methods of training had proved somewhat less than efficacious in the training of the hound. Holmes, a master of the flexible training methods approach, sat the dog, placed meat in front of the hungry dog and sent the dog forward, making the animal break the sit position with the command, 'Go on'. Holmes increased the distance the dog was required to go to reach and eat the meat and finally set out the meat before the training session sending the greyhound forward in the required direction to seek the meat. It was a clever adaptation of a method – a system Holmes apparently used to train many dogs after his success in training his greyhound to an incredible standard of obedience.

Net steadiness is always a terrifying section of the training of a long netter's dog – at least as far as the tyro lurcherman is concerned. In point of fact, getting a dog steady to the nets – not to snatch the quarry from the net – is relatively simple. Firstly when a rabbit or hare strikes the net the creature struggles a second or so and then, as the meshes of the net encompass them, it ceases to struggle and remains still. This stillness, this near-comatose condition is biologically useful to the species as predators are often baffled by the attitude of their entrapped prey – playing possum explains the attitude of a trapped beast when a predator approaches it. Hence while the dog that is starting to learn skills to assist the long netter may mouth the odd rabbit or so at the start of the season, as the season progresses the excitement of the dog for the netted rabbit wanes and the command, 'No', will usually stop the dogs mouthing rabbits. I hasten to add that at the very start of the season I always expect my best dogs to make the odd mistake or so when working long nets or with ferrets and purse nets.

Long netting is usually practised after dark but I always train my lurchers to nets of any sort during the daylight hours. After dark the mistakes the puppy makes can only be realised when the deed is actually perpetrated and the sound of toppling nets and enmeshed, struggling dogs alerts the lamper to the fact that all is not well. During daylight hours the long netter is able to watch a dog start out on the path to making a mistake and correct that mistake before the dog becomes enmeshed or the rabbit damaged by the dog mouthing it.

I start training a puppy to work with a long net by netting large burrows, ferreting the burrows and allowing the rabbits to bolt fairly unencumbered by purse nets but restricted by the long net that surrounds the warren. When rabbits high-tail it to the nets and the young lurcher follows on the heels of the rabbit the long netter is able (if, that is, the puppy has been trained to a high level of obedience) to stop the youngster crashing into the nets – and, reader, a fifty-pound lurcher hitting nets at a velocity of something like thirty miles an hour will cause considerable damage to the nets and sometimes to the dog. A few weeks of working in daylight and driving rabbits, or rather, seizing rabbits that refuse to tangle in the nets and return to the burrows, will usually convince the youngster that the nets and the quarry tangled in them are forbidden.

I confess I have attempted to teach several dogs to work to the long net by introducing them to the activity during the hours of darkness, but I have experienced little success and what success I have obtained has been due to the dog becoming so terrified as a result of misadventures in the meshes that it is too frightened to approach the net. I once trained a collie (an early attempt at producing a merle coloured, true breeding, working bearded collie) to drive to the long nets for a warrener/handyman/gardener who worked for a local estate. My sole knowledge of teaching such a dog had been gleaned from books concerning the exploits of Victorian poachers who taught their cur bred lurchers the skills during the hours of darkness. By the end of the month the bitch seemed upset when the warrener reached for the bag that held the nets and I realised I had made a mistake in the training programme – a mistake I never succeeded in rectifying, I should add – for the animal was terrified by her numerous tangles with the nets my associate had set up. Since then I have never introduced a dog to the art of long netting during the hours of darkness. Handlers that are able to see the problems a dog is encountering are able to forestall and correct those errors.

It is policy to sit a dog alongside the net that is being set up and to walk the dog near the long net before it is sent to drive the field. Any method that prevents a collision of dog with those nets is useful but it would surprise the reader to realise how easily a dog taught that entrapped rabbits and nets are forbidden during daytime training sessions will ignore the nets at night.

A surefire recipe for disaster during a long netting spree is to work two dogs together – even if the dogs are used to each other's presence. Once the element of jealousy enters the hunt and the dogs start to compete with each other to catch game it is only a matter of time before complete and utter chaos develops – game is ragged, nets are torn or forced down by the impact of lurchers striking them. I literally detest working two dogs together, even kennel mates who have grown up together, and when a fellow hunter cajolingly requests if he can bring Ben/Gyp along my teeth are set on edge. Nothing but nothing ruins a lurcher more certainly and more permanently than hunting the lurcher as part of a team.

May I end this chapter and, indeed, end this book with a simple statement — if a lurcher is to be trained properly it must enjoy a one man, one dog relationship with its owner. Mobhanded hunters with a dozen lurchers on slip achieve virtually nothing when attempting to train a lurcher. At the time of writing I own two trained lurchers and one long dog — I am woefully over-dogged!